Creating Ideas

Discover Writing Topics
in Daily Life

Gayle L. Watson

Gayle L. Watson

DEDICATION

To the writer in all of us!

Published by:
City Life Books, LLC
P.O. Box 371136
Denver, CO 80237-5136
U.S.A.
www.citylifebooks.com

Requests for such permissions may be addressed to:

Gayle L. Watson
c/o City Life Books, LLC
P.O. Box 371136
Denver, CO 80237-5136
U.S.A.

Copyright © 2004
First Printing 2004

ISBN 0-9746860-2-6

TABLE OF CONTENTS

WRITING YOUR MISSION IN THIS WORLD
Choosing Your Format

Introduction

You're ready to write something, so you sit down and prepare to start. But you are drawing a blank as to what to write about. Congratulations! You are not alone. While the reasons are numerous as to why writers draw a blank on a topic, the end result is the same. A blank page. My mission is to help you tap into the wealth of information in every day sight. This book will give you a variety of ideas in which to brainstorm topics.

I have talked to many students who say they haven't done anything interesting in their life. I have heard from a girl who is fifteen years old, and she says she has no experiences to write about. Do you know what I have to say about that? Bull Hockey!

Have you ever heard the phrase, "write what you know"? You know lots of things. You may not realize what you know right now. I will teach you how to look around and recognize it.

We'll start small and go from there. You will be surprised how much information you already have stored inside of you. At the end of each section is an exercise to complete on your own to ensure you are able to apply the technique learned in the section. Based on the examples given, there shouldn't be another utterance of "I don't know what to write about."

This book also includes a section on how to generate an entire topic from one part of an idea. You may have a favorite place or favorite person to write about. We'll take the singular idea and build from there.

After the topics have been formed, this book will take you further down the path to selecting a good topic based on the writing assignment. Many writers have topics that are best suited for research assignments but have difficulty coming up with good topics for creative assignments. We'll discuss how to choose based on the mission at hand.

You will discover very quickly how to turn on the tap and watch the ideas flow out. And once you discover how easy it is to uncover these ideas, you will never be at a loss again. Read on. You'll never look back.

LOOKING AT YOUR WORLD

ON THE INSIDE LOOKING OUT

The first part of this book deals with creating ideas within four-walled rooms. It is my purpose to expand those four walls, allowing you the freedom to explore the potential contained within. I believe that after you complete these exercises, you will no longer see a room, but a world of possibilities.

BEDROOM

The logical place to start is the bedroom. It's a place you see at least once a day. Dreams are formed, tears are shed, the future is mapped out, and your individual expression is presented here. Some of you may have to share your bedroom with a brother or sister. If so, have you ever drawn an imaginary line down the middle of the room to mark your territory? It's human nature to be very possessive of your space. After all, this is an extension of your personality.

Some of you may write in your bedroom. Library books may be spread across the floor and the bed to complete a homework assignment. There may be a spiral notebook with the words "My Diary" written on it and tucked into a dresser drawer. You may be writing in your bedroom, but you aren't writing about your bedroom.

I'm going to take you on a tour. Your bedroom is a reflection of you, right? There must be at least one idea this room can generate.

Step One:

Close your eyes and picture your bedroom. Do you see it in full color? Are you including obvious items like the bed, dresser, and clock radio? If you have a computer in your room, skip it as an entire section is devoted to this item later in the book.

Step Two:

How vivid is your imagination?

Is there a time on the clock radio? Do you remember what color the trash can is?

If details like these don't appear in your immediate recollection, don't worry. By the end of this book, you will be a certified topic detective! You'll learn that even the smallest detail can provide a starting ground for developing an idea.

Step Three:

Now that you've got a clear mental picture, go look at the actual room and see how good your memory is. You may be surprised that you forgot to include a poster on the wall, or the green stuffed frog by the door.

Step Four:

Pretend you are a visitor walking into this room for the first time. What is the first thing that catches your eye? Is it your bed, a poster, a chair, or an incomplete science paper?

The reason it catches your eye may vary. It could be due to the size of it, a sentimental memory, a bad memory, or purely because it is located directly in front of the door.

Step Five:

Take out a piece of paper and start taking notes. Write down everything you see and leave space after it for comments and questions.

Be sure to look at specific items. Note the colors of the walls, type of bed, or is it a mattress on the floor? Are you listing pictures on the walls, books or magazines, time on the clock, curtains or blinds on the window, and even the lint on the carpet?

I'm starting off with the first thing that catches my eye in my room.

Why? Being able to single out one item as an idea is the easiest way to create topics. All of my attention is focused on one thing.

Cedar Chest

I stand at the doorway of my bedroom and the cedar chest is the first item to catch my eye. It jumps out because it's right in front of the door, I notice the detailed craftsmanship, and it's a family heirloom filled with memories.

The cedar chest was my grandmother's. She traveled with it across the country years ago. It had already been packed full of a lifetime when it came to me. There were handmade quilts inside when I moved it to my bedroom.

I write down the idea "cedar chest" on the page and list a series of questions under it.

- ✓ When did my grandmother get it?
- ✓ Was it a present on her eighteenth birthday?
- ✓ Was it a wedding gift?
- ✓ Who gave it to her?
- ✓ Was it empty or were there a few household items in it?
- ✓ What was the first thing she put in it?
- ✓ Did she use the quilts?
- ✓ Do I still have the quilts inside?

I need to investigate it further. I clean off the top and lift the lid.

I am immediately reminded of why it is called a cedar chest. There is no mistaking the sharp acrid smell of cedar trees. It's amazing how the smell has yet to fade after all these years. I root through the few items inside and realize I have never put any of my belongings in there.

Being a good topic detective means I have to question everything.

- ✓ Why haven't I put my own items inside?

I write down possible reasons.

- ✓ Is it a sacred place?
- ✓ Do I not want to intrude on my grandmother's space, even if she died years ago?

Nah, I have taken the chest for granted for the last several years. Placing my items in it hasn't even occurred to me until this very moment. Besides, if I wanted to use something stored inside, I would have to air it out to get rid of the odor. The odor works though. Years ago someone realized cedar trees were a natural bug deterrent.

I shut the lid and inspect it further. The key has long since been lost.

- ✓ Where is the key?
- ✓ What treasures could have been locked inside?
- ✓ Was this innocent piece of furniture used to hide secret items?

Visions of moonshine bottles lined up inside it fill my mind. My grandmother would have never broken the law, or would she... I laugh at the thought and refocus back to the current day and ask myself this question.

✓   How does the cedar chest fit in my present day room?

I have a CD player and humidifier sitting on top of it. There are CDs scattered around. I have a couple of framed snapshots cluttered in with the CDs.

Each night I change out the CD and pour water in the humidifier. Until this moment, I had forgotten the history and beauty of it. The chest has become nothing more than a functional piece of furniture in my bedroom.

Look around your room and see if you have a piece of furniture that has some history to it. It may be a dresser that an older sibling used. Perhaps it came from a garage sale or estate sale. You can look for clues from the previous owners and develop your own series of questions that lead to writing topics.

Topic Detective Time

I have investigated the idea of the cedar chest and asked several questions about it. I have come up with these topics that could be used to write an assignment. Later I can decide if these topics are better suited for research assignments or creative assignments.

- ✞ Who discovered the scent of cedar as bug control?
- ✞ Is this the reason a cedar chest was invented?
- ✞ What do other people keep in their cedar chests?

Laundry Basket

I scan the room for another idea and stop at the pile of dirty clothes in the laundry basket.

I recall a commercial on TV about how the smell of a shirt can transport the person back to a party the night before. I have the ability to sort through my own dirty clothes and see if the same experience happens to me.

I decide against it. The only time I want to sort through smelly laundry is when I'm sorting the whites from the colors. Instead, I opt to observe from where I sit on the floor. I write down the idea of "sweat pants" next on the page.

- ✓ Where did I wear them?
- ✓ Whom did I see?
- ✓ Why was I wearing sweats and not jeans?

It's true! I am transported back to the snowy day, the cold walk to the store, and the three boys throwing snowballs at a car. They saw me just as they threw a round of snowballs. They were busted!

- ✓ Who were they?
- ✓ Do they play baseball in the summer?

I am stumped as to what else to say about the sweat pants. I lose interest writing about the laundry basket. It seems like I always have dirty clothes. I realize this is probably why the sweat pants topic turns cold quickly.

Don't get caught up in one direction with an item.
Three areas of ideas come from the sweat pants. I
could write about the actual pants, the memory of
when I wore them, and, because they are in the laundry
basket, I can write down laundry-related items.

Remember, every comment or question on paper is
important. The more you have written down, the better
your chances are you'll find an interesting topic. If you
discover the item to be quickly uninteresting, move on.
There are plenty of others to investigate.

Topic Detective Time

I have investigated the idea of the laundry basket and
asked several questions about the sweat pants inside. I
have come up with these topics that could be used to
write an assignment on. Later on I can decide if these
topics are better suited for research assignments or
creative assignments.

- ✦ How many times does the average person
  change his clothes each day?
- ✦ What is the most popular laundry detergent?
- ✦ Three best friends make snowballs one day.

Shoes

Next, I see a tennis shoe half sticking out of the closet
door. I have big feet. I know I have big feet. My size
eleven shoes have a hard time staying in the closet.
I write down "tennis shoes" and open the door. I look
at the pairs of shoes randomly tossed on the floor of
the closet. I reach in and take out a black chunky one.

These were a special pair that I bought to go with an outfit. I went to Las Vegas with some friends. I was wearing this great outfit and shoes when I got the guys at the Venetian to give me a kiss on each cheek. One of my friends took a picture. To this day, it's one of my favorite pictures.

Unfortunately, the shoes hurt so bad, I wore them once and never again. I find the memory of the blisters on both feet coming back. I subconsciously start rubbing my foot at the same spot where a monster blister had appeared. I toss the shoe back in the closet and frown.

✓ Why do I still have these shoes?

I rifle through the other pairs of shoes and remember another shoe story.

My family and I went camping and stopped in Arizona. The campground owner told us to leave our shoes outside of the zipped tent. At night, scorpions like to come out and find dark places to crawl into. The owner told us to shake out our shoes when we got up in the morning. If a scorpion had taken residence in one of our shoes, once shaken out, they would scurry off to another hiding spot.

I have two older brothers. Need I say more? There were no scorpions in our shoes, but I was so paranoid at the thought. My brothers took every opportunity to scare the daylights out of me.

I started off with one shoe, but moved on to another. Don't focus solely on one item. If there are related items in the area, write brief notes on all of them. You can go back later and pick your favorite from the list.

In addition, don't miss an opportunity to recall a personal memory or adventure. By choosing a topic based on first-hand experience, you can include a variety of personal details.

Topic Detective Time

I have investigated the idea of shoes, asked several questions and recalled some personal shoe-related memories. I have come up with these topics that could be used to write an assignment on. Later on I can decide if these topics are better suited for research assignments or creative assignments.

- ✦ What is the largest shoe size?
- ✦ What is the smallest shoe size?
- ✦ What is the average?
- ✦ What causes blisters?
- ✦ What is the best cure for blisters?
- ✦ How long does it take for the average shoe to be "broken in?"
- ✦ Does a certain type of shoe cause blisters more often than others?
- ✦ Camping in Arizona and desert critters that come out at night.
- ✦ My camping trip to Arizona with my family.

Blue Hippopotamus

I turn around to see what time it is. Since I am in topic mode, I survey the surrounding area. A blue hippopotamus is staring back at me. I got the hippo from a friend years ago. I don't really know why he gave it to me, but I still have it.

I hold it up and blow the layer of dust from it. Dust remains in the creases of the blue rubber form. I try to scrape it out, but give up. There is a clear outline on the dusty clock radio from where it has been sitting for months. No, probably years. It still squeaks when I squeeze it.

I obviously still have some attachment to it or I would have gotten rid of it. I look at the clock radio every day, but the hippo has become invisible. I decide to place it back on the clock radio, making sure it is in the same spot. He has probably long since forgotten he gave it to me.

I decide not to write about it.

Never forget, there are some things you can keep to yourself. You always have the choice in deciding what to write about.

Rocking Chair

I choose one last item in my bedroom. There is a rocking chair in the corner, covered in stuffed animals. The rocking chair has no nails in it. It was completely constructed with wooden pegs in the early 1900s by a distant relative. No one is exactly sure which distant relative. The finish on the chair makes it look like dark wood. It's really made of light oak, but the finish has hardened and darkened over time.

If I had the motivation, I could refinish the chair back to the original look. I run a finger across the layer of dust on this as well and realize it hasn't seen a spritz of Lemon Pledge in quite some time.
I write down "rocking chair" and some notes.

✓ Which relative made it?
✓ Did they make other pieces of furniture?

I write down "stuffed animals" next on my piece of paper and take them out and look each one over.

✓ Where did each one come from?
✓ Why did I decide to keep them all these years?

There is one animal in a plastic bag. He's still in the bag as he's a collectible. Should I ever decide to sell him on eBay, he'll be worth more if unopened.

I don't play with any of them. In fact, they are covered in a layer of dust as well. I should really look more into dusting my room. It appears I'm severely lacking in this area of cleaning.

I wrap a teddy bear from my childhood in my old baby blanket. It's an old soft blanket with satin trim around the edges. The bear looks awfully cozy in it. I arrange the rest of the stuffed animals in the chair.

✓ Is my little sister jealous of my collection?

In this example, I take one large item, the rocking chair, and break it into two items. By going through the contents of the chair, I am able to generate an

additional idea and turn it into topic questions. You
can do this with dresser drawers, jewelry boxes, and
shelves on the walls.

Topic Detective Time

I have investigated the idea of the rocking chair and
added stuffed animals as an idea at the same time. I
have come up with these topics that could be used to
write an assignment on. Later on I can decide if these
topics are better suited for research assignments or
creative assignments.

- ✦ How long ago did wooden pegs stop being used
  in furniture construction?
- ✦ How does furniture refinishing get done?
- ✦ Why do people collect stuff?
- ✦ What do people collect?
- ✦ How much of a price difference is it opened vs.
  unopened?
- ✦ What is the history of stuffed animals?
- ✦ Where is the largest stuffed animal collection?
- ✦ What is the highest valued stuffed animal?
- ✦ What do these stuffed animals do when I'm not
  home?

Conclusion

I have chosen a variety of items that are very average in
most bedrooms. You will find that you have items in
your bedroom that have specific memories, historical
memories, or a unique appeal that is representative of
your personality.

I started off with the easiest way to generate ideas. All I needed to do was look around a room. Once I focused on a specific idea, I wrote down the object name and then came up with several questions, comments, and stories about the idea.

I call this the *LIST* process. List everything you can find in the room. Write comments and memories about the ideas on the list. The best way to generate topics is to write questions about the idea. Your topic may live in answering the question.

- ✓ Where did it come from?
- ✓ Why do you have it?
- ✓ Do you represent the national average of an item or activity?
- ✓ How is it made?
- ✓ What is it used for?

Your topic may also live in recalling the memories and stories surrounding the idea.

- ✓ I caught three boys throwing snowballs.
- ✓ Scorpions could have crawled into my shoes while camping.

You can use these as a starting place to generate writing topics. Create your own storyline using a memory as the inspiration. This process can be used in any room to identify ideas and generate topics.

LIST Exercise

For this exercise, go into a brother's or sister's room. Ask for their permission first! If you have no sibling, go into the guest room or to a friend's house.

1. Try and list everything you can from your memories first.
2. Go into the room and look around.
3. Now, write down everything you see.
4. Fill in the missing details from your original list.
5. Pick out five items on your list that interest you.
6. Think of one research question (i.e., How old is this?) and one creative question (i.e., What if this was in my room?) for each of the five items.

You should be able to come up at least one topic to write about after you complete this exercise.

FAMILY ROOM

They say the heart of every house is the kitchen. It's where people congregate, food is prepared and served, and it's the warm memories in a cold winter and cool memories in a hot summer. I guess they mean when you stand in front of the open refrigerator door! I want to challenge that comment and say the family room is the heart of every house.

The family room is a place where family portraits hang on the walls. It is where you and your date go on Friday night to eat popcorn and watch creepy late night movies. This is the meeting place for many families to sit and talk to each other.

I have been in family rooms full of sports equipment, listened to piano lessons, watched hockey games, and hung out with friends until midnight on New Year's Eve. Every home has one.

Step One:

Go to the family room in your house. Take a seat and look around the room. Does it feel comfortable? Can you kick off your shoes and put your feet up? I hope so.

Step Two:

Look at how the furniture is arranged in the room.

Step Three:

Look at the pictures and the family projects in the room.

Step Four:

Look at the audio visual equipment.

Step Five:

Write down what interests you in this room. Don't list each item you see, but write down your favorite pictures, favorite chair, favorite movie, only the things that mean something to you.

I sit down and kick off my shoes. The first thing I make note of is the furniture placement.

Television

There are two chairs and a couch that face both each other and the TV.

The TV is the most important thing in the room. I spend way too much time watching it, and I couldn't live without it. Yet, it isn't so important that my furniture face it completely, but they also face each other so conversations can take place (probably about what is on the TV!).

✓ Since the TV is practically another family
member in most households, does it get treated
like one?
✓ Why do I love TV so much?

I watch TV when I'm bored, when I'm tired, when I'm
lonely, and when I'm walking on the treadmill. There
are times when the TV is on, but I have no idea what
program is playing. I like the sound in the background.
This makes me wonder if I am representative of the
average TV viewer. I don't think I want to compare
myself against other viewers. I like the TV and I'm not
changing my habits!

Next to the TV is a cabinet with some DVDs in it. This
is a great topic to write about. You can talk about your
favorite actors, favorite movies, directors, highest selling
DVD, and the first DVD you ever got.

I count up my paltry number of DVDs. I don't seem to
watch movies over and over again except for a few. I
notice that some of them are still wrapped. They have
never been opened or watched. I blow the layer of dust
off of them.

✓ Where did I get these DVDs?
✓ Will I ever watch them?

Okay, I just had the thought of re-gifting. You know,
where you receive a gift, but don't want it, so you re-
wrap it and give it someone else. Cheesy, but it's a
thought.

✓ Who can I re-gift this DVD to?

I then sort them by genres. I seem to like dramas the best. I only own one comedy. This says something about my taste.

✓ When renting DVDs, who gets to pick them out?

TV is more than entertainment. It is now a staple in virtually every household. Here is an opportunity to ask questions and write about how it fits into your home life. It is the most important item in my family room.

Topic Detective Time

I have investigated the idea of television. I have come up with these topics that could be used to write an assignment on. Later on I can decide if these topics are better suited for research assignments or creative assignments.

✦ Do most families watch TV together or are there other TVs in the house?
✦ How many hours does an average family watch per week? Are you average?
✦ Do families plan their schedule around TV shows?
✦ How many households fight over what show to watch?
✦ Who controls the remote?
✦ How many family members talk back to the TV?
✦ How many homes have a DVD player? More than one player?

+ Average number of DVDs owned by an average household
+ Who buys the DVDs?
+ What is the most popular type of movie?
+ What is the least popular?
+ What do girls like versus guys?

Music

I move on to my CDs. I have way too many to sort. Instead I make a few notes about the ones I haven't listened to in years and the cabinet in general. It's covered in a fine layer of dust. Note to self: I need to dust! I then remember the ones I listen to are upstairs in my bedroom on the cedar chest.

✓ Why does someone stop listening to a CD and move onto a new one?
✓ Who listens to the CDs in your house?
✓ Where do you listen to CDs in your house?
✓ Do you crank up the music in the family room when no one else is home?

Writing about musicians, types of music, and favorite songs can make interesting topics. How many times have you been hollered at to turn down the music? I loved getting my first set of headphones. There were no more shoes hitting the bedroom door. That was our family code to turn it down. With headphones I could tune out all the other sounds around me.

Topic Detective Time

I have investigated the idea of music. I have come up with these topics that could be used to write an assignment on. Later on I can decide if these topics are better suited for research assignments or creative assignments.

- ✦ What makes music classic?
- ✦ How many CDs does the average person buy a year?
- ✦ How have computers changed this?
- ✦ Do certain songs remind you of a place or experience?
- ✦ How do your music tastes compare to a sibling?

Magazines

Even though nothing can compete with the TV, I do on occasion engage in other media in the family room.

There are stacks of magazines. I need to give those away. I hate tossing them out, so they are stacked high. It has become my new hobby. Let's see how high they can get before they slide off into a pile on the floor. I get my yardstick and see that they are two and a half feet deep.

- ✓ If I opened ten magazines, what ad would I see the most?
- ✓ What magazines get fought over in a family?
- ✓ What is your favorite magazine?

I have a magazine that I've kept for the last several years. It has a checklist of one hundred things to do in life before you die. I have made it my personal mission to attempt doing all of those things before I die. So far, I only have about one third of them checked off. I find myself reading some of the articles in this magazine over and over again when I look at the checklist.

Topic Detective Time

I have investigated the idea of magazines. I have come up with these topics that could be used to write an assignment on. Later on I can decide if these topics are better suited for research assignments or creative assignments.

- What do other people do with old magazines?
- How many people hang onto magazines?
- Check eBay for magazine auctions.
- What is the most popular magazine subscription?
- How long is the average story in a magazine?
- What article subjects are timeless?
- What grade level do most magazines write at?
- Do people reread magazines? If so, why?

Projects and Pictures

There will be some discussion about pictures later on in the *Computer* section of this book. However, I will talk about other ways to look at pictures here.

There are formal portraits of various family members on the wall. Some include cousins, aunts and uncles, while others are of brothers and sisters only. There aren't any photographs or amateur snapshots in here. I wonder why since this is the family room? Wouldn't it make more sense to have the fun vacation pictures or silly poses from a party in this room? The formal ones seem so, well, formal. This doesn't fit with my image of a laid back family oriented room.

✓ Do you find the same portraits on your walls?

The other items noted are the projects made in school or at camp that adorn the walls. My mom hung a decorated piece of tree bark I made in girl scouts camp on the wall in her house. It was the silliest piece of wood, but she was proud of it. Mom always made sure that my siblings and I were well represented.

Of course, my cat statue that I made in 8th grade is displayed in the family room.

✓ Why did I make a cat?
✓ Why would this be displayed in this room and not in the kitchen?

Parents love to show off their kids by displaying their pictures and crafts. Think about your grandparent's house. Is your picture on their wall?

Topic Detective Time

I have investigated the idea of portraits and projects. I have come up with these topics that could be used to write an assignment on. Later on I can decide if these topics are better suited for research assignments or creative assignments.

+ What kinds of projects are displayed?
+ Do kids make items specifically for this room of the house?
+ Do any projects represent the entire family?
+ Does having a fireplace make a difference?
+ Do these items blend in or do they stand out?
+ At what age do the projects stop being made?
+ Do the projects reflect an era?
+ Are pets considered part of the family?
+ Do they have their own furniture?

Family Matters

Okay, we are talking family here. How many fights have gone on in the family room? I have seen guys jump over the couch with a glass of water aimed at a sibling. I have seen arguments break out over who gets to use the car next. Many of these discussions seem to take place in this room.

✓ Who gets to pick the next TV show?
✓ Who gets to control the remote next?
✓ Why didn't you tell me who you were going to prom with?
✓ I'm never talking to you again.
✓ I hit a fence, but not very hard.

All of these conversations have taken place in my family room. Do any of them look familiar? Even though the moment is heated with debate, fear, anger, or argument, the family room comfort bounces back and family members congregate in it the next day.

Topic Detective Time

I have investigated the idea of family matters. I have come up with these topics that could be used to write an assignment on. Later on I can decide if these topics are better suited for research assignments or creative assignments.

- ✦ What has been the biggest discussion in your family room?
- ✦ Is it easier to talk in the family room?
- ✦ Whom do you fight with in the family room?

Conclusion:

Family is about conflict, love, hope, anger, frustration, peace, and every other emotion. Any story or paper that discusses any aspect of the family is already filled with history, emotions, and drama. Drawing from any family memory can be a good topic to write about.

The family room is a source for memories and activities. Even something as simple as watching the TV can become a full idea when the family is involved. I call this the *FAMILY* process. By focusing on the physical items in this room, the emotional attachment to them or to the room itself can be tapped into.

FAMILY Exercise

Go into the family room or family room equivalent in
your house.

1. Find an object that has an emotional meaning
    to you. It may be a school project, a picture, a
    baseball glove from the game the day before...
2. Write that object down on your paper.
3. Write the story or circumstance surrounding
    the object.
4. Write down who was involved in the story.
5. Write down your family's response to what
    happened.

You may decide to write about more than one thing in
this room. Remember if you should chose to write
about a family event, you can always base the idea on
your experiences, but create different details.

KITCHEN TABLE

Have you ever thought about your kitchen table? No, I'm not going to list all the fabulous foods that have graced the surface. If I did, I'd be running to the fridge. Instead, I'm going to give you a different formula to create writing ideas.

Many families eat in front of the TV, on the run, or outside of the home. If this is the case in your house, what the heck do you need this flat round, square, or oblong surface for?

Traditional house floor plans continue to include space for a table, so why not have one. There are a couple of holidays each year that include events surrounding the table where family and friends do visit from time to time. It could be that you are the exception and actually eat meals at your table on a regular basis.

I sit down at my table and look around the kitchen. Boring. Appliances. If you find some fascination in GE or Whirlpool, you may want to look it up and do a research paper on it. Then I see the dirty dishes in the sink. Ugh... It's time to move on to the second way of creating ideas.

Step One:

Sit at your kitchen table and think about every activity you have ever done here besides eating. Part of this exercise is to go back as early as you can remember.

Did you come up with some activities? Did you come up with at least one from your childhood?

Step Two:

Take out a piece of paper and start writing down the activities.

If you find you are stumped, don't worry. In this section we will talk about several activities. Let's see if this will help you create some of your own ideas.

Parties

I sat at my table one time and called up a group of friends. I had their phone numbers laid out, a checklist of who was coming and who wasn't, and the grim reaper theme. I told them the date, to wear black clothing, and that it was a surprise birthday party. They were sworn to secrecy as the party plans progressed.

The food was arranged on the table. The birthday cake was placed right in the center and had black frosting on it. The number "twenty-one" was in bold white letters. Everyone showed up and was my friend surprised! We had a contest to see who had the blackest tongue in the crowd.

I have also planned informal Friday night movie fests featuring our favorite movie star.

I decide to note all the facets of planning a party.

- ✓ Who should I invite?
- ✓ Where should I have it?
- ✓ Is it a surprise or not?
- ✓ What kind of party is it?
- ✓ Whom did I plan it with?
- ✓ What kind of food and drink?

Of course, I have to ask one of the obvious questions about parties.

- ✓ Why do people congregate in the kitchen during parties?

This is a good opportunity for you to write down some memories from specific parties that could be good topics to write about.

Topic Detective Time

I have investigated the idea of parties. I have come up with these topics that could be used to write an assignment on. Later on I can decide if these topics are better suited for research assignments or creative assignments.

- ✦ How often are surprise parties really surprise?
- ✦ Do all countries celebrate birthdays?
- ✦ Where did the birthday cake tradition come from?
- ✦ What is the most popular type of party? Why?

Games

My brothers and I had an ongoing game of Monopoly
for weeks at a time. We always ran out of cash and
ended up using white paper with dollar amounts
written on it. We met at the table same time each
afternoon and battled it out. I never won a game, but I
was good competition for each brother.

I remember being very young and playing Go Fish. I
had to kneel on the chair to reach across the table. I
remember this card game as I learned what fifty-two
card pick up was that day. I think the jack of diamonds
never turned up again after playing my brother's game.

I don't miss those board games. At least on a computer
game, it can't cheat or talk you out of your Monopoly
money!

Topic Detective Time

I have investigated games as an idea. I have come up
with these topics that could be used to write an
assignment on. Later on I can decide if these topics are
better suited for research assignments or creative
assignments.

+ What is the most popular board game or card
  game?
+ Where do they rank in sales of all games?
+ Has their popularity decreased? If so, what
  took their place?

Friends

I have sat at this table on several occasions and had morning coffee with friends. I love the way the morning sun comes in through the patio door and makes it a bright cheery place to talk. We have been known to spend hours sitting around the table talking about clothes, guys, and food. Since the kitchen can be a high traffic area, our conversation can be interrupted with my brother bringing in grease loaded hands from working on his car, or his friends.

- ✓ How much traffic flows through your kitchen?
- ✓ Does the conversation get interrupted a lot?

The kitchen table is a place to meet at late night as well. My brother and his girlfriend broke up at midnight over the table. His first clue was when she sat down at the furthest end of the table from him.

- ✓ How late do friends stay?
- ✓ What are the conversations usually about?

Topic Detective Time

I have investigated the idea of friends. I have come up with these topics that could be used to write an assignment on. Later on I can decide if these topics are better suited for research assignments or creative assignments.

- ✦ What effects does the sun have on a room?
- ✦ Is there a psychological impact?
- ✦ How important is it to gossip?

✦ Is the table important to dating?

Christmas

This topic could be divided into numerous subtopics. I tried to keep the focus on activities done at the kitchen table only.

During the holiday, the kitchen table is covered in newspapers with paper towels on top. There are stacks of warm chocolate chip cookies, sugar cookies, bon bons, chocolate crinkle cookies, gingerbread boys, and oatmeal raisins cooling. We always have a baking factory over one weekend. One day we bake, the next day we frost and decorate all the cookies. For some reason, my mom always thought the cookie recipes should be quadrupled. It was a task to frost fifty snowmen-shaped sugar cookies.

The memory of baked cookie aromas wandering through the house always transports me back to being a child.

✓ How old was I when I first got to frost the cookies?

Each family has some type of holiday cookie tradition. Think about holiday cookies that are unique to your family.

Wrapping Christmas presents is another holiday table activity. The bags of paper, bows, ribbons, and name tags sit on the kitchen floor for the month of December. We pick a time when the other family members aren't around and wrap like crazy to get it done.

✓ Do family members help wrap presents?

The table has always been a family destination in December. As kids we would make ornaments or popcorn balls, my mom would always have a special tablecloth on the table. While the table is a functional piece of furniture, it is a part of the family during the entire holiday season. Any holiday can generate additional activity around the kitchen and kitchen table.

Topic Detective Time

I have investigated one holiday, but any others could be substituted as an idea. I have come up with these topics that could be used to write an assignment on. Later on I can decide if these topics are better suited for research assignments or creative assignments.

- ✦ What traditions do families have on the holidays?
- ✦ What special recipes have been handed down over generations?
- ✦ What are the annual sales of Christmas paper?
- ✦ What color ribbons and bows are the most popular?
- ✦ What is the strangest wrapped present?

Homework

There were times I would do my homework in my bedroom. But the floor would get hard, my bed would be too soft, or I would get distracted by wanting to do other things in my room. If I had a big paper to work on, I would often sit at the kitchen table. The formality of sitting in a chair at the table surface seemed more like a classroom setting and I could concentrate better. I also found that if I were studying for a test, usually another family was around and I could ask for help or get quick answers to questions instead of looking them up. Mom was always good at knowing answers.

- ✓ I wonder if my mom made me do homework at the table when I was a kid?
- ✓ Did I get better grades when studying for a test at the table?

Not only have I written school papers at the table, but I've also written letters, books, notes, papers, journals, articles, grocery lists, to do lists, goals for the future, and memories of the past at this flat piece of furniture. My laptop is sitting on it right now as I type this sentence.

- ✓ How many authors who have disclosed their writing habits included the kitchen table?
- ✓ How many books have been written at the kitchen table?
- ✓ How many reports, letters, or other items have been written at the kitchen table?

Topic Detective Time

I have investigated homework as an idea. I have come up with these topics that could be used to write an assignment on. Later on I can decide if these topics are better suited for research assignments or creative assignments.

+ Where is the best place is to do homework?
+ How popular is the kitchen table as a place?
+ Do family members help or hinder homework?
+ Where else do people write in their house?
+ Why do people write at the kitchen table?

Family Meetings

I have discovered that most family meetings happen in one of two places, either in the family room or at the kitchen table. At least this was the case in our family. I remember being at the table and my mom spreading out the map and brochures of our next family vacation. She would show us the route we would travel and then match up the brochures highlighting the events we would do once we got to our destination. That was a good family meeting.

Not all family meetings were positive though. We also got the news of my parents divorce at the kitchen table. There was really no place to hide, unless I crawled under the table at the time. I guess I could hide my sweating palms at the news of what this change would bring us. The kitchen table was never really the same after that family meeting.

✓ Parents and students map out college choices at the table.
✓ Wedding invitations have been written out.
✓ Boxes of photographs have been sorted through and put in albums or sent out.

Topic Detective Time

I have investigated family meetings as an idea. I have
come up with these topics that could be used to write
an assignment on. Later on I can decide if these topics
are better suited for research assignments or creative
assignments.

- ✦ Why do families meet at the table?
- ✦ Does a family react differently at news brought
  to the table or in the family room?

Storage

Boxes have sat on my table until a fine layer of dust
covers them. Piles of junk mail have sat on my table.
No one ever sits at the end, so why let a perfectly good
flat, sturdy surface go to waste? Once I get tired of
looking at the stuff, I go through it and toss out the
majority. I have to admit that the treasures found in
boxes can be great topics. I completely forget what is in
them until I force myself to clean up the clutter.

If you happen to have boxes sitting on your table, take
a look inside them and see what treasures you have
sitting there.

- ✓ Is it a fruitcake from grandmother last
  Christmas?
- ✓ Is it a car part that is for the wrong year of
  automobile and it needs to be returned?
- ✓ Did you forget to mail in the order form for
  pizza at the next soccer party?

Topic Detective Time

I have investigated storage on the table as an idea. I have come up with these topics that could be used to write an assignment on. Later on I can decide if these topics are better suited for research assignments or creative assignments.

- How many households store important documents on their table?
- How often are important documents forgotten because they were in a pile on the table?
- Do families keep valuables (jewelry, cash, etc.) in piles on their kitchen table?

Conclusion

What I have done in this section is take one idea, the kitchen table, and uncover topics based on it. I chose the kitchen table as many of you may only think of it for one purpose, but, as we discovered, a multitude of activities can be associated with it.

Listing activities is more involved than listing objects. Since there is an action involved in each topic, the questions or personal history regarding these activities can produce a more complex background.

I call this the **_MULTIFUNCTION_** process. By removing the obvious usage of an item, it can be an adventure in recognizing our various adaptations to it. This can be applied to many items around your house. Be creative and see if you can identify others.

MULTIFUNCTION Exercise

1. Go into the garage.
2. If you don't have a garage, go sit on the couch.

Garage Exercise

1. Take away the obvious use of parking the car in this space.
2. By looking at all the items in the garage, come up with five other uses for the space.
3. Come up with one childhood experience in the garage.

Couch Exercise

1. Take away the obvious use of the couch as a place to sit.
2. Think of every item you've ever placed on the couch.
3. Come up with one childhood experience that included using the couch.

Were you able to create one topic from this exercise?

Did you come up with building a go-kart (or some other construction) in the garage?

How about building a fort using the couch?

COMPUTER

The popularity of the home computer has evolved into an area on its own. Some homes have a main computer set up in a central location like a home office or den. Others have it set up on a kitchen counter, or a desk in the corner of the family room, and, perhaps, a filing cabinet alongside it. Many of you have a computer in your bedroom.

This space has taken on a life of its own. In this exercise we are going to look at the computer and surrounding area and generate ideas based on the clues this space reveals about the user's personality.

Step One:

Sit down at your computer and relax. Get a feel for the space around you. Is it in a corner of a bedroom? Or is it in a an open area, like a room for a home office?

Step Two:

Now that you've taken a moment to become aware of your space, think about the purpose of it. Do you do homework at it? Do you share it with others? Do your parents run a business from it? Do you use it only to surf the net, blog, or play games?

Step Three:

Look at any toys, pictures, and hobby related items that are yours. If you do share it with others, only take note of your items.

Step Four:

Last, I want you to think about the items on and around your computer. Do they stimulate creativity? Or do they distract from getting homework done?

Step Five:

Get out a piece of paper and list all of the personal items in your computer space/desk area. If you have a bookshelf, computer stand, printer stand, shelves, bulletin board, or file cabinets, include everything personal on these items as well.

This is not an exercise to remind you of homework assignments, this is about the personalization you have brought to your computer area.

What if you have nothing personal?

Hard as it is for me to believe, I actually know a family where their computer sits on a desk in the family room by itself. There is a box of tissues sitting next to the mousepad and that's it! If you are in a similar position, this section may not be of interest to you.

I think the majority of us fall into the personalization category. I'm starting off with some of the most common items found on my desk.

Vacation Pictures

Vacation pictures top my list. I have magazine pages torn out for Mexico and the Scandinavian countries of Norway and Sweden. I have planned weeks of activities and places I want to visit when I travel there one day. I am constantly updating the pages when I come across a new one on the internet. There are places on my wall where the pictures are three pages deep.

I love looking at the ocean and scuba diving pictures in Mexico. Sometimes, I spend hours dreaming of the perfect water, perfect fish, and diving with the perfect dive buddy.

I have other pictures on my desk of places I have actually gone to. There is one of a campground fire with my friends huddled around it in our coats. Each time I look at that picture, I feel a chill. It was so cold that night, I could barely feel my toes in the morning.

We all want to escape and we want to remember the moment we did.

- ✓ What is the best vacation I've been on and why?
- ✓ Where would I recommend my friends go?

Based on the pictures I have up, I can tell that my personality runs both cold and hot! I want to go to Mexico to scuba dive and I want to go to Sweden when it's cold and see the Fjords and ice skate. The mountain camping trip also follows this theme. It was sunny and warm during the day, but freezing cold at night.

Look at your vacation pictures and see what clues it says about you. Write down any themes or similarities in the places you dream of going to or places you have gone to. You may discover places you have gone to were a favorite in your family.

Topic Detective Time

I have investigated the idea of vacation pictures. I have come up with these topics that could be used to write an assignment on. Later on I can decide if these topics are better suited for research assignments or creative assignments.

- Why do people like to go on vacation?
- What is the most popular destination?
- Do they select the destination based on weather?
- Do they select the destination based on what activity can be done there?
- How many people go back to the same destination again?
- Who takes cruises versus flying to a destination and driving with a map or taking a formal tour?

Family Pictures

Family pictures are also popular around the computer. I have one of my cats sitting on top of the monitor. Yes, my cats are part of the family. I also have a picture of my human family. None of these are formal pictures, but snapshots from vacations and birthday parties.

I now have to wonder what family pictures say about me.

- ✓ Do I have a favorite brother or sister? Why?
- ✓ What is my favorite family vacation? Why?

Don't forget about the cyber pictures and include those in your list. My desktop picture is the cats and my screensaver is a variety of vacation pictures of California, my cats, and my family. Well okay, and I have a few pictures included of my favorite hockey players.

Clues left behind in pictures can tell if you are a world traveler, family person, or animal lover. Topics can be generated about the picture itself, and also about the person who has them displayed.

Topic Detective Time

I have investigated the idea of family pictures. I have come up with these topics that could be used to write an assignment on. Later on I can decide if these topics are better suited for research assignments or creative assignments.

✦ How many families consider their pet as a
   member?
✦ Do pets go on family vacations?
✦ How many screensavers are set up to show
   pictures of the family and their pets?
✦ Is one family member shown more often than
   another?
✦ Why is one family member shown more?

Hobbies

One of my biggest passions is clearly displayed at my
desk. I have all my hockey items scattered on the walls
and on my desk. I love the fast pace of skating and the
skill involved in making those incredible plays. My
favorite item is the Patrick Roy poster of a great save he
made while playing with the Colorado Avalanche.

Anyone who comes up to my desk for the first time will
know immediately which sport is my favorite. What
does this hobby say about me? I list some questions
that could be asked.

✓ Do I spend time daydreaming about my
   hobbies instead of working?
✓ Are these hobbies family related?
✓ When did they become hobbies and why?
✓ Is it on the screensaver or desktop of my
   computer?
✓ Is my mouse pad a reminder?

Exploring the beginning of a hobby can be a fun
adventure. Think back to the first time you discovered
it and the events surrounding it. Then look around

your desk and see how well it is represented. Hobbies not only show a person's interests, but they may show a person's intensity level, age, and popularity with friends.

By going through your hobbies, you can tap into a wealth of information. Since you enjoy the particular activity or subject, you will be able to write with enthusiasm about it as topic.

Topic Detective Time

I have investigated the idea of hobbies. I have come up with these topics that could be used to write an assignment on. Later on I can decide if these topics are better suited for research assignments or creative assignments.

+ Do people who like hockey like to ice skate?
+ Is hockey more popular with men or women?
+ Where does the popularity of hockey rate in all sports? Am I part of the crowd?
+ How much space is taken up with hobby related items?

Inspiration and Motivation

I have a framed copy of the "what I learned in kindergarten" message. I read it often and find that I never get tired of reading it over and over again. When you walk down the halls of your school, you may see an eagle flying with a phrase underneath it to encourage you, or something similar. I have noticed that many schools have prints or sayings on their walls.

✓ Are they in teachers' offices?

Even if you don't read it each day, the message is still
there. When I look at my computer space, I have to
ask why I have this message up. It inspires me and
reminds me of the important things in life. Sometimes
I need to remember to not sweat the small stuff.

✓ Where did I get it from?
✓ Was it a gift?

I think I did get it as a gift. One of my friends
recognized that I can be intense at times and worry
about all the small details in life. This is a reflection of
my personality.

There are numerous posters and prints that have
motivational, inspirational, and success related sayings.
Are there any motivational prints or sayings on coffee
cups, plaques, or other items on your desk or around
your computer? Do you look at them often or do they
blend in the background? Take a moment and read it
if you have one up. Remember, your environment
affects your creativity. Anything that assists you in being
creative, use it!

Topic Detective Time

I have investigated the idea of inspirational and
motivational items. I have come up with these topics
that could be used to write an assignment on. Later on
I can decide if these topics are better suited for
research assignments or creative assignments.

✦ What is the number one stressor in school?
✦ Do these motivational prints work?
✦ What personality type is more likely to have them displayed?

Sound

I have a clock radio on my desk. I've had it for years. The clock no longer works, but the radio does. Every time I sit at my desk the first thing I do is turn on the radio. I know people who can't concentrate when there is any other noise in the background.

✓ Do I really listen to the radio, or does it ramble on in the background?
✓ Does music assist me creatively?
✓ Does music make me work faster because the beat of a song is fast?

I know a girl who lives in a large city. She loves to open the window and listen to the street noise. She likes the distraction of sirens on police cars and fire trucks. She says it helps her imagination stay active. At times, she will wonder where the emergency vehicles are going and she creates an entire storyline based on what she hears going on outside.

While observing with your eyes in an area is one way to create topics, using all of your senses can assist as well. If you find you are a personality who becomes very focused on a game or document on the computer screen, try and break free from the screen. Close your eyes and listen for a moment. Then make a mental note about your reaction to it. Do you feel more relaxed? Surprised at what you hear? A waste of time? Ask yourself what this says about your personality.

Topic Detective Time

I have investigated the idea of sound. I have come up with these topics that could be used to write an assignment on. Later on I can decide if these topics are better suited for research assignments or creative assignments.

- ✦ Who likes quiet versus who likes noise?
- ✦ How important is it to have noise when working?
- ✦ What kind of music do people study or work to?

Trophies, Awards, and Diplomas

One of my proudest moments was college graduation. It took me a few years, but I finished it and have several pictures of the graduation ceremony in full display to remember my moment! The smile on my face is wider than the Mississippi river.

I also have an award that I won for my writing on the wall. Some of you may have trophies in sports, awards in art class or certificates for completing a program.

- ✓ Do you have these items on a shelf or hung on the wall? If not, why?

All of these items give clues to the person who uses this space.

- ✓ Am I goal-oriented?
- ✓ Do I still like the sport/subject that I won in?
- ✓ Is it related to a hobby that I have?

If the wall or shelf is covered in trophies or awards, question what it says about your personality, and don't be shy about your success! It took hours of your life and dedication to earn any kind of certificate, diploma, or award. Displaying it at a place where you study can assist you in accomplishing new goals.

Topic Detective Time

I have investigated the idea of awards, trophies, and diplomas. You don't have to limit it to these items. I have come up with these topics that could be used to write an assignment on. Later on I can decide if these topics are better suited for research assignments or creative assignments.

- ✦ Which fields require degrees?
- ✦ How much does an average college degree cost?
- ✦ What is the most popular degree?
- ✦ How many students go on to get masters and doctorate degrees?

Decoration

I have a set of science fiction planet prints. I don't know the artist or what planets they are supposed to be.

I just like the way they look. There is something peaceful about the colors used in them and the idea of space being a quiet reflective place. They match no other pictures on the wall. They don't even match the color of paint on the walls. There was something about them that caught my eye.

The time and money spent on decorating a computer space can give clues to a personality in a topic.

I have seen desk spaces that are institutional clean. A surgeon could operate on the desk top. I have also seen desk spaces where the desktop was buried under a mountain of books, papers, clothes, CDs, and pictures. Would you rather have a messy but comfortable space, or a clean and orderly space?

There are some people who want this area to state their personality in bold colors. They spend time in front of their computer each day and like to look at friendly surroundings. For others, it is a functional area to work on the computer. Which one are you? Your computer space will give away numerous secrets about your personality.

Topic Detective Time

I have investigated the idea of decoration. I have come up with these topics that could be used to write an assignment on. Later on I can decide if these topics are better suited for research assignments or creative assignments.

✦ How much time does the average person spend
    decorating their computer space?
✦ What are popular decorations?
✦ What are the most expensive decorations?
✦ What does a clean desk say about the person?
✦ What does a messy desk say about the person?
✦ Are scientific thinkers more likely to have
    matching decoration?
✦ Are creative thinkers more likely to have non-
    matching decoration?

Conclusion

So as you can see, my office is loaded with more
personal memorabilia than my bedroom. If you have a
desk in your bedroom, many of these items may be
duplicated on that list. Don't worry if it is. You can
never have too much information.

What have you just learned about yourself? It is likely
this is the place you will spend more time than any
place else. Most people like to surround themselves
with memories of home, fun things, creative things, and
things that serve as recognition of hard work.

You may have never been aware of the clues you leave
out for others to show what motivates you, keeps you
entertained, have personal meaning to you, but in
looking at all of these items, a different set of ideas may
be discovered.

I call this section the ***PERSONALITY*** process. By
focusing on the relation of the items in an area, a good
topic detective can learn a lot about a person and
develop story ideas, character ideas, or research ideas.
Linking these items together create a complete picture.

PERSONALITY Exercise

Go to a friend's computer space and ask them for permission to complete this exercise.

1. Note the personal items.
2. Group the personal items together by sports, pictures, music, knick-knacks, pets, etc.
3. Take those items and list some assumptions (i.e., hockey fan, dog lover, art student, or world traveler)
4. Pick out one item and decide why you think they have it on their desk.
5. Write down a personality trait that makes this item individual (i.e., educated, athletic, intense, organized, compassionate, angry)
6. Come up with two questions about the personality trait.

Are you able to create one topic from this exercise?

If not, find one thing you have in common in both of your areas and write down why you think that is.

SCHOOL DAYS

We spend years in school. Each classroom has a
different feel to it. The type of class that is taught and
the grade level affects this feeling. Some rooms have
rows of desks, others tables with chairs, and rooms like
science or art will have specialized furniture to match
the subject.

There are classrooms that have windows, while others
are located on the interior of the building or in the
basement. Even though a classroom may have
windows, the blinds can be closed. The teacher doesn't
want the student to be distracted.

The walls of a classroom speak volumes. Elementary
school walls are a symphony for the senses. They
proudly display the art work created by the children.
Fun poems with cartoon characters run down a
hallway. Brilliant rainbows and clouds are painted on a
classroom wall.

Schools cater to the stimulation for young minds and
support the self esteem of the children. I'm sure
students have proudly shown the outlines of their
hands to anyone who wants to see them!

I have always found it interesting how high school
science room walls are usually covered as well. There
are pictures of planets, the periodic table, posters of
great scientists, full color pictures of plants and flowers,
and sometimes a volcano or two.

By the time we get to college, there are no more
pictures on the walls. Each classroom is a generic copy
of the room next to it. We're lucky if we get to see an
advertisement for an upcoming theatrical production,
or a rally for a social or political cause led by a school
group.

We are left to create all on our own. I suppose the
hope is that we can tap into our youthful days and
recapture some of that elementary school energy.

In this exercise we are going to locate some of that
energy and turn it into writing ideas. You will learn how
to take a patchwork memory and develop it into a full
topic.

Step One:

I want you to think about all of the classrooms
you've been in during your school lifetime.

This may result in nothing more than an
assortment of patchwork images from
different schools and years.

Step Two:

List each image that comes to mind. Don't get
caught up on trying to remember the details.

Your list may not include anything more
substantive than a listing of school names,
classes, teachers, a picture or poster on the

---

wall, the name of a student you sat next to, or a specific project you completed.

If you have memories of a school activity, list it as well. The purpose here is to get as many details on paper, whether they are complete or not.

Step Three:

Go through your list and separate out the good memories from the negative ones.

Pick one item on your list and write down everything you can think of about it.

If you struggled with listing thoughts related to your chosen memory, this section of the book will help you.

Pottery

I attended an art class every day for a year. The majority of those classes are a collective blur, but I remember one day in particular. We worked with clay.

I had a lump of brownish-gray clay that I was able to mold into a cat statue. Each student had their own creative idea in how to make their lump a personal piece of art. This was the only time I ever worked with clay, but I liked the hands-on creativity.

- ✓ Why haven't I done this again?
- ✓ I wonder if they still teach this in school?
- ✓ What type of clay did I use?

Had I not had this one exposure to pottery in school, I would not have been able to think of topics about this.

If the incident is a negative memory, can you trace how it may have affected you today? Have you avoided the subject? Or have you made some other decision based on the experience?

Topic Detective Time

I have investigated the idea of pottery. I have come up with these topics that could be used to write an assignment on. Later on I can decide if these topics are better suited for research assignments or creative assignments.

- What different types of clay are used?
- How do glazes work?
- How competitive is the pottery world?
- Where does a student go to school for this craft?
- How much training is required to find a full time job in this field?
- Why do people work with clay?
- What is the history of pottery?

Poet

We had a guest speaker once in an English class one day. He jumped around the room, spouting poetry with each breath. His passion for poetry was infectious.
It was late that night and I ended up sitting at my computer and writing until early morning. It resulted in

some of the best words I had put on paper the whole semester.

Instead of focusing on the poetry I wrote, the topic detective in me was more interested in the reasons I was charged up from class.

- ✓ Was this an adrenaline rush?
- ✓ Does an inspiration like this cause better quality writing?
- ✓ What was it that charged me up?

If you get a "rush" from a class, go with it and write, or paint, or work out math equations. By going with the flow, you can start a foundation. The next time you come back to the work at hand, there is something to work with. You may be able to tap into the inspiration once again.

Topic Detective Time

I have investigated the idea of a guest speaker and the adrenaline rush it caused. I have come up with these topics that could be used to write an assignment on. Later on I can decide if these topics are better suited for research assignments or creative assignments.

- ✦ How does adrenaline work?
- ✦ How can we recognize true passion versus false pretenses?

Mold Experiment

I have clear memories of growing mold specimens in a science class. Each week we would look at our slice of bread and see whose sample was moldier.

I kept my class notes from this class. Even though I didn't win the mold experiment, it was fun to recall all the information we kept on a piece of bread! Oh right, there is a difference between mold and fungi.

✓   I wonder where that piece of bread is now?

I realize I have to check my refrigerator and see if any mold experiments are growing. I find that I'm actually excited to see if there are any! The fridge is clean, but I'm buzzing with excitement about this recently rediscovered topic once again. Why? I remember the experience of learning about it.

The teacher's class presentations came to mind. Had the teacher only given lectures on mold, my interest would have been in finding a comfortable position to sleep in his class. The same is true with generating topics.

Presentation is important. If you try to force a topic on paper and don't have the concentration to complete it, the reader will recognize your lack of interest. If you can't think of an exciting way to present it, move on to another topic. You will have a surplus of topics created from going through this book.

Looking At Your World   School Days

Topic Detective Time

I have investigated the idea of mold and fungus as
science experiments. I have come up with these topics
that could be used to write an assignment on. Later on
I can decide if these topics are better suited for
research assignments or creative assignments.

- ✦ Why are hands on experiments more
  interesting than lectures?
- ✦ How important are field trips to the museums?
- ✦ Do long term projects make a class easier or
  harder?
- ✦ What is the difference between mold and
  fungi?
- ✦ How long does it take for mold to grow?
- ✦ What is the best environment to grow it in?
- ✦ What is the difference between black and green
  mold?
- ✦ How much does refrigeration slow down mold?

Group Projects

Group activities were noted several times on my list.
Since they occurred in different classes and at different
school levels, I made a separate category for this idea.

- ✓ Would you rather have individual projects?
- ✓ Do you like group projects?

Okay, who really likes group projects? Really... Some
slacker's not pulling his weight and the rest of you have
to make up for it since the grade is based on the group.
I note this as a negative experience.

68   Creating Ideas – Discover Writing Topics in Daily Life

I'm not a great fan of promoting negative words in life, but when you come across a topic that crops up in several different places as a bad memory, don't ignore it. There are reasons why group projects exist and ways to explore this topic from an interesting angle.

I would argue group activities from a negative point of view based on my experience, but I would not make the paper one sided. If you feel strongly about a topic, make sure you present a balanced paper. By offering both sides of a topic and drawing from all types of examples, you can make a convincing case.

Topic Detective Time

I have investigated the idea of group projects. I have come up with these topics that could be used to write an assignment on. Later on I can decide if these topics are better suited for research assignments or creative assignments.

- ✦ What is small group interaction?
- ✦ Are two heads better than one?

This set of topics works with the set of questions that prompted it.

- ✦ Does taking a test as a group result in a better grade?
- ✦ How does a fire department work?
- ✦ Is it safe to scuba dive alone?

I came up with these group topics by asking myself the question "who?"

✦ Who <u>wants</u> to work as a group?
✦ Who <u>has</u> to work as a group?
✦ Who <u>needs</u> to work as a group?

Classmate

During one grade in elementary school, I sat next to a kid named Brad. I have a vague memory of his face. I don't know why I remember him, but every now and then I wonder what happened to him.

My gut feeling tells me he was a nice kid. I have no reason to think he teased me as a child. But I am perplexed as to why I can't remember more about him.

✓ Who was Brad?
✓ Why do I remember him?
✓ What class was he in?
✓ What school was he at?

By going through these questions I am able to come up with the teacher's name, school name, and the grades we were in class together at the same time.

Since I don't know the answers to the rest of Brad's life, I decide to question the blanks I would have to fill in on my own.

✓ Did he go to college?
✓ What is Brad doing today?
✓ Where does Brad live today?
✓ Does he have a family?

I now have the flexibility to write my own conclusions about Brad's life. I can use this information to create a character in a story, create a storyline, or write a mock grade school reunion.

Topic Detective Time

I have investigated the idea of classmates. I have come up with these topics that could be used to write an assignment on. Later on I can decide if these topics are better suited for research assignments or creative assignments.

+ Why do people remember one student and not another?
+ How often are grade school classmates remembered?
+ How many people go back and visit their grade school?
+ Why do people go back?

Conclusion

This section is more abstract. You will need to rely on the belief that what you write down has some significance or you wouldn't remember it. Once you have a list, you can then sort out the topics that you want to question and write about them.

I call this the **_EXPERIENCE_** process. If you have a clear memory, build on it and develop a complete thought. Without a clear memory or action available, brainstorming the odd events surrounding the patchwork of images can bring some topics to light.

EXPERIENCE Exercise

Pick a recent memory or item from your last year of
school. Think of a class.

1. Write down everything you can recall from the
    class.
2. Listen to your gut. Was the experience good or
    bad?
3. Question the surrounding items, teacher,
    subject, city and state of the school, other
    students, class project, etc., and see if a more
    complete memory develops.
4. If not, use the information you do have and
    write a fictional answer to the remaining
    questions to complete the idea (i.e. a student, a
    class, a subject, a teacher, an art object)
5. Write two topics from a perspective that fits
    your feeling of it. If it is a happy memory, write
    with a positive tone. If it is a negative memory,
    write it from a constructive angle, presenting
    both sides.

If the only thing you can come up with is a poster on
the wall, or one art object completed, go with it. Try
and list as many items related to that one idea.

ON THE OUTSIDE LOOKING IN

In this section you have the opportunity to look inside a physical space, like a car, or a personal space, like observing a person during a bus ride. You will be on the outside looking in. It is more challenging to keep up with a world that is in constant motion.

RIDING THE BUS

When I take public transportation, I sit and watch the people around me. I always bring a book with me, but I never open it. I am too interested in those sitting around me and what is happening outside.

Being up high in a bus gives the rider an excellent opportunity to look down into the car sitting next to you in traffic. I'm sure you have looked into a car alongside you in traffic while on the school bus. I am always interested in what people have in their car, if the car is clean or messy, and what the driver is doing besides paying attention to the road.

Step One:

While on the school bus, be a topic detective on your next ride.

If you haven't ridden or take the school bus, try a short public bus ride for this exercise.

Of course, the public transportation experience is always unique based on the route the bus travels and the time of day you go. Find a route with a good mix of commercial and residential neighborhoods. Pick a time to ride during rush hour traffic.

Step Two:

Make notes throughout the bus trip of everything you see out the window.

I recently rode the bus and took notes for this section of the book. You will learn how to uncover ideas in a world that is in constant motion around you. Being able to focus on one item and take quick notes is important as the bus continues to move down the road.

Outside Workers

There were two men putting up a new billboard. It was a full sheet of some material that was being attached to the billboard. Both men seemed very adept at moving around the tiny scaffolding and putting the new ad up.

- ✓ What do they see up high in the air?
- ✓ Did they have to get used to the height?

I noted several different jobs people were doing outside. On this trip I spotted construction workers, utility workers, landscapers, and a tow truck driver. I never realized how many people work outside. I wonder how many people driving notice them or do they blend into the background? You can generate a similar list of job-specific questions about each worker you see outside.

Topic Detective Time

I have investigated the idea of outside workers. I have come up with these topics that could be used to write an assignment on. Later on I can decide if these topics are better suited for research assignments or creative assignments.

* What is the history of billboards?
* How high up are they?
* How are billboards done today?
* How do they decide where to put them up?
* How much does it cost to run an ad on a billboard?
* How much do billboard workers make?
* How many signs can they do in a day?

Automobiles

The bus was at a red light when I heard a man yelling at his son. Several people on the bus looked up since the man was in a convertible and the top was down. He was yelling loud enough for the entire block to hear. The boy's head hung low, his shoulders slumped over while the man yelled. The second the light turned green, he sped off.

✓ Didn't this guy realize everyone could hear him?
✓ Maybe the boy wasn't his son?

Even without the benefit of knowing the entire story, you can certainly make some assumptions based on the information at hand. Take this opportunity to create your own story based on the questions raised by this scenario.

You can build the background as to how it got to this point, and you can fictionalize the reasons behind it.

Topic Detective Time

I have investigated the idea of automobiles. I have come up with these topics that could be used to write an assignment on. Later on I can decide if these topics are better suited for research assignments or creative assignments.

- ✦ Where were these two going?
- ✦ How many fathers and sons argue in the car?
- ✦ How many people believe the outside world doesn't notice them in their car?

Characters

The bus moved on to the shopping mall. We stopped next to the parking lot and waited at a bus stop for a couple of minutes before leaving. I watched a woman load up her trunk with two arms full of bags.

- ✓ What was in the bags?
- ✓ Was it for her or her children?
- ✓ Was it for a birthday?

What I love about this observance is you can use your imagination to create anything in those bags. She may look like an average woman on an average shopping trip, but what if she isn't...

Another character was the woman pumping gas at the gas station. She was in a short skirt. Her bright red sports car grabbed the attention of those around her.

✓ Why kind of person likes to drive bright red sports cars?

Without the benefit of known information, I wondered if she had three kids waiting for her at home. I wasn't close enough to see how old she was, and for all I knew, she could have been a grandmother.

People create stories within themselves. By their actions or their appearances, we may compare them to someone we know, or categorize them into a stereotype. By drawing from our backgrounds of similar types of people, we can create an idea based on their presentation and our personal experience of similarities.

Topic Detective Time

I have investigated the idea of characters. I have come up with these topics that could be used to write an assignment on. Later on I can decide if these topics are better suited for research assignments or creative assignments.

✦ Who is this person?

✦ How much time do these people spend on
their appearance?
✦ What are they doing?

Advertising

I then noted the guy on the corner dressed up in the
oversized paper cup to advertise a sandwich shop.

✓ Can they really see out of those things?
✓ How long is their shift?
✓ How hot does it get inside?
✓ Do people honk at them?
✓ Do you wave back?
✓ Throw things at them?

Put yourself in the oversized cup's shoes for a moment.
Think of what a passenger in a passing car may do.
Sure you can include some mean things, but be
creative and think of the weirdest question or action a
person in a passing car may have done. Maybe the car
was stopped at a red light and they just went to the
grocery store, so the passenger handed the oversized
paper cup person a can of soda. Sounds silly? It could
be a story.

Topic Detective Time

I have investigated the idea of advertising. I have come
up with these topics that could be used to write an
assignment on. Later on I can decide if these topics are
better suited for research assignments or creative
assignments.

✦ What is the craziest advertisement you've seen?
✦ Who comes up with these ideas?
✦ How do they brainstorm these ideas?

Recreational Vehicles

I noted an older couple in a recreational vehicle. They
were stopped at a gas station. Both were in their late
60's, I'd guess. She was in bright new clothes for the
trip. He was mopping his brow with a handkerchief
and pumping gas.

✓ Where are they were going?
✓ To see the grandkids?
✓ Were they members of AAA?

I am transported back to my own childhood. My family
had a travel trailer for years. This couple looked way
too happy. We were three miserable kids, trapped in a
tin can going down the highway. No TV! It was terrible!

Camping trips, RV travel, anything that involves the
term "road trip" is worthy of a story.

Topic Detective Time

I have investigated the idea of recreational vehicles. I
have come up with these topics that could be used to
write an assignment on. Later on I can decide if these
topics are better suited for research assignments or
creative assignments.

✦ How much has RV travel changed over the
   years?

- ✦ Where do people drive to the most?
- ✦ How long do people stay?
- ✦ Do people set up RVs for parades, picnics, sports events or concerts in lieu of getting a hotel room? What is the strangest event?

Conclusion

This is an easy exercise in observation. If you don't have access to public transportation, put a note pad and pencil in the car. When you have the opportunity to ride as a passenger, look out the window. See what's going on outside. By asking everyday questions, several ideas can come to mind. You may even want to talk it over with the driver of the car. I know if I had been in the car with another person, I would have commented on the girl and the sports car. I suspect several questions would have been generated between us upon seeing her.

I call this the *OBSERVATION* process. By being a silent observer in a bus or car, the world outside is going about its business. You get a front row seat to it, if you stop and take notice. The best observations are made about people. If you'll note, all of my comments here had to do with people and their actions. I found that if I looked at buildings, I wondered who was inside and what were they doing? If I looked at cars I wondered who was driving them and where were they going.

OBSERVATION Exercise

Ask a friend to drive while you observe as a passenger.

1. Write down comments about buildings, cars, people, or anything interesting that catches your eye.
2. Choose a colorful or interesting person you see out the window and observe them closely. List at least two details about the person.
3.   Select two of the most interesting items that catch your eye. Write down at least two questions for each of them.

Select one item of interest and ask the driver to make some mental conclusions about it. Write down your own conclusions.

As an example, if there is a car full of people, ask the driver to make a mental note of where they think the people are going while you write down where you think they are going.

After you have written your idea, ask the driver what his thoughts were. You may be surprised by how the driver answers. Add it to your topic collection.

DRIVING

Have you ever noticed how little kids notice and question the smallest details? I own the same kind of car as a friend of mine. A six year old child got into my car for the first time. He immediately noticed my car was the same as hers, but not exactly.

He looked around and commented on how the other car is green, but mine is blue. He pointed to the front seat and said the other one had one seat across the front, but my car had two separate seats.

Although I had been in both cars numerous times, I never took a moment to step back and really notice the details. If we could transport ourselves back to being a six year old and question the world with new eyes, we wouldn't have to work through this book to create ideas! Every experience would be a new piece of information to question and learn from.

Cars are always a good topic to write about. The auto industry tracks every detail of car sales across the country.

- ✓ Which style sells more?
- ✓ Bench seats or bucket seats in the driver's row.
- ✓ Which color sells more?
- ✓ Which color is more involved in accidents?
- ✓ Which color is more popular with families vs. with singles?
- ✓ Which color appeals to what age group, or perhaps by section of the country?

Historical data about cars can be researched and
analyzed in a paper. But, what if you are more
interested in the story the car tells? In this section we
are going to create ideas based on where the car has
been.

Step One:

Go outside and look at your car or your
family car. If you don't have one, ask a friend
or relative. List all of the outside details,
including the bumper stickers, decals, dirt, tire
wear, any clue that the car gives you about the
driver's habits or previous owner's habits.

Step Two:

Look at the accessories on the car. See if the
car is equipped for off-road adventures, city
driving, or for presenting a specific style.

Step Three:

Next, get inside the car and sit down. Look
around and list everything you see inside it.

Are you surprised at the details you have already
gathered? Cars can be a story all by themselves.

Exterior

This is the first impression a car makes. When looking
at cars in a used car lot or on the road, many

impressions are formed based on the style, color, and
condition of the car. Besides the basics, look at the
individual markings outside.

- ✓ Any radio station stickers?
- ✓ Is there a license plate frame naming a
  dealership or interests of the owner?
- ✓ Any music group decals?
- ✓ Are there any school parking stickers?

I always wonder what the driver of a car does when I
see their government sticker allowing them access to an
armed forces base.

Some cars look like they've had a rough life. They
seem sad with chrome molding hanging off the side, a
headlight not lined up quite right in front, or the roof
dented from a hail storm.

- ✓ Does the car look like it was in an accident?
- ✓ Did anyone get hurt?
- ✓ Did snow or rain cause it?
- ✓ Did the driver fall asleep?

Topic Detective Time

I have investigated the idea of a car exterior. I have
come up with these topics that could be used to write
an assignment on. Later on I can decide if these topics
are better suited for research assignments or creative
assignments.

- ✦ Create a journey for the car. Start off with the
  assembly line in Detroit, imagine a life on the

✦ road, people the car has transported, and how it
  finally ended up in your driveway.
✦ What types of exterior accessories attracts the
  most attention to a car?
✦ Where is the mudiest place to drive a car?
✦ What's the difference between a 'cool car' and
  an 'old car'?

Interior

What does the inside of the car tell you? Some obvious
signs clues can determine if a family drives the car.

✓ Are there smashed up cookies/crackers in the
  back seat?
✓ Are there potato chip bags and soda cans on
  the floor of the back seat?
✓ Are there backpacks, school projects, or
  papers?
✓ Is there soccer equipment?

Perhaps the car is used for business as well as personal
travel.

✓ Are there company brochures inside?
✓ Are there electronic supplies or other business
  related items?

I remember when I bought a used Jeep Cherokee. It
was only a few years old, but it had high mileage on it.
When I folded down the back seat, I found a golf ball
hidden under it. I came to the conclusion that the
previous owner was probably a sales person who drove

a lot of miles for work and entertained clients by playing golf.

I decided the two door, red model was ideal for a young salesman who also enjoyed sports. I wondered what he sold and did he only use the hatch back for loading golf clubs, or were there other items stored in the car.

One small golf ball created a person and a use for the car. Don't overlook any item.

What about the carpet? Has the car been vacuumed lately or is there an adventure in the upholstery. You may discover more clues about the car and where it's been.

- ✓ Is there dried grass and dirt?
- ✓ Is there sand from the beach?
- ✓ Is there dog hair?

Topic Detective Time

I have investigated the idea of a car interior. I have come up with these topics that could be used to write an assignment on. Later on I can decide if these topics are better suited for research assignments or creative assignments.

- ✦ What does the interior smell of a car say about the owner?
- ✦ What kind of driver hangs items from the rearview mirror?

✦ How have pet carriers evolved for traveling animals?

Trunk

Trunks are a great place to generate ideas. They can be closed tight hiding a world of sins, or a wealth of supplies.

Is the trunk clean? My grandparents were very well prepared for driving. They had a box containing jumper cables, wool blankets, an emergency flashlight, maps, an umbrella and road flares. My grandfather always used to remind me that driving was a privilege and one should always be prepared.

✓ How many people drive around with laundry in it?
✓ Who keeps woofers in their trunk?

The trunk is another good example of a multifunction object. Some people practically live in their cars. They keep numerous household items inside their trunk.

Topic Detective Time

I have investigated the idea of a car trunk. I have come up with these topics that could be used to write an assignment on. Later on I can decide if these topics are better suited for research assignments or creative assignments.

✦ What is a good supply kit for the trunk?
✦ How safe is it to store things in the trunk?

✦ What was it originally invented to be used for?
✦ How could one build a swimming pool in their trunk?
✦ What is the strangest item found in a trunk?

Glove Box

I have a map in the glove box. Did you open the glove box and look inside? Does anyone keep gloves in their glove box these days?

Like the trunk, the glove box is another place to hide something. Many cars have locks on it to keep items secure inside.

✓ What is kept inside one?
✓ How long has the package of chewing gum, or a roll of Life Savers been there?
✓ Are there items from the previous owners tucked into the corner of it?
✓ Does your car have a glove box?
✓ What kind of music cassette tapes or CDs are inside?

You may be surprised at the forgotten treasures tucked inside the glove box. An idea or two may be at your fingertips.

Topic Detective Time

I have investigated the idea of a car glove box. I have come up with these topics that could be used to write an assignment on. Later on I can decide if these topics

are better suited for research assignments or creative
assignments.

- ✦ Why is it called a glove box?
- ✦ Travel back in time to 1950 and create what
  items are contained in the glove box.

Conclusion

Now that you've listed all the items outside a car and
inside a car, you can come up with a determination of
where the car has been. I call this the **_DESTINATION_**
process. It's not about the car itself, but about the clues
that lead you to see what the car is used for, other than
driving, and where the car has been in its travels.

For some cars the destination may be no further than
taking the dog to the vet. For other cars, the destination
may be climbing the side of a mountain and camping in
the wilderness for weeks. Using all of this information,
you can draw your own conclusions and write about
them.

DESTINATION Exercise

Go to an older sibling or friend's car. Pick a vehicle that you know very little about and ask the owner for permission to be a detective.

1. First look at the outside of the car. Note all details about the paint, condition, markings, tires, etc.
2. Make a separate note if you detect damage from being in an accident. This topic can provide a whole list of ideas on its own.
3. Pick two details that you have noted and write down at least two conclusions regarding those details.
4. Next get inside the car and look around. Note all details about the upholstery, items contained inside and clues about the use and history of where the car has been.
5. Pick two details and write down at least two conclusions regarding those interior details.

Create your own story line about where the car has been and why. You may decide in this exercise that you would like to a research paper on autos as opposed to creating a storyline.

CREATING YOUR WORLD

PARTS OF A WHOLE

This section of the book is about taking one important element of any paper and developing it into a full idea. There are many pieces to writing a good story, but I feel the three main components are character, setting, and plot.

CHARACTER

Characters are many times the foundation of a story. If your audience can relate to the character, the character will live in the readers' minds for years to come. We, as readers, love to finish a story and laugh at the character because we realize we may be easily laughing at ourselves.

You may know a family member, school friend, or brief acquaintance that has a crazy personality or unique hobby. You may also recall a "character" you saw on the street a month ago. If they stand out in your mind, there is a good reason. They did something, or were someone, different or interesting.

You will want to focus on a person that stands out in your mind for this section of the book. If you do not have a specific "character" in mind, the second part of this section will help you create a character to start your idea. This section is a little different from the last. All of the information gathered will lead to one set of topics at the end.

Step One:

Think about an unusual or unique person in your life. Picture what they do, what they are wearing, when it is, any detail you can remember about them or the activity that stood out.

Step Two:

List their personality traits.

Step Three:

Write down why they would make an interesting character. Is it something they've done, where they grew up, or why they behave in a manner that is different?

I picked an individual that I knew for several years. She has remained in my memory all this time as I have never met another girl quite like her.

To refresh my memory, I start off by listing all of the details about her I can remember.

- ✓ She grew up in a warehouse in Montana.
- ✓ The warehouse belonged to her uncle.
- ✓ She had seven brothers and sisters.
- ✓ One of her brothers made music videos.
- ✓ She starred in several of the videos.
- ✓ She was bulimic.
- ✓ She owned a dog, I think his name was Max.

Next, I write down some personality traits.

- ✓ She was a free spirit.
- ✓ She was always in a good mood.
- ✓ She was never on time.
- ✓ She never worried about "the small stuff" in life.

Now I list why she is a good candidate for a character.

- ✓ Her childhood is unusual in where she was raised.
- ✓ She has starred in music videos.
- ✓ She has obvious health concerns.
- ✓ It is apparent in knowing her that her personality has depth to it.

Since I don't have all the details, I will have to fictionalize pieces of the story. If I choose to write non-fiction, I have a starting ground in which to focus my research on.

In order to generate some topics based on her background, I ask questions to brainstorm different directions. I break apart these questions into three main areas.

Childhood

I decide to start in the beginning and work on where she came from.

- ✓ Why didn't she live in a house?
- ✓ How long did she live in Montana?

- ✓ Were all of her brothers and sisters living with her?
- ✓ Or did some live on their own and not in the warehouse?
- ✓ What did her parents do?
- ✓ Were they married or not?

Sibling Relationship

I focus on her relationship with her one brother. Out of all of her siblings, why did she stay closest with him?

- ✓ How did he get into music videos?
- ✓ Who was in his band?
- ✓ Did she follow him out of Montana?

Bulimia

The topic of bulimia contains a host of angles.

- ✓ Do other bulimics who come from the same type of family background?
- ✓ Is her happy personality a result of her disorder?

Topic Detective Time

Now that I've established some background on this "character," I have several writing topics developed that could be research papers or inspiration for a creative paper.

- ✦ This could be a story about growing up poor in Montana.

✦ This could be a story about family strength and how her uncle came to the rescue.
✦ This could be a piece about music videos and the popularity of local bands.
✦ This could be another family angle of how a brother and sister worked against the odds and forged a new path through music.
✦ Is there a connection between Montana and bulimia?
✦ This could be a story about how a brother helps his sister in the battle of bulimia.

Conclusion

Building a topic around a specific person doesn't mean you need to recreate their life. You want to take pieces of their uniqueness and use it to create an interesting character from them. Sometimes characters are a mixture of several different people. You can mix and match background details from your favorites and create a new character.

As you can see in this example, only having a small collection of details can grow into several topics that are both related to research and creative writing.

Creating a Character

If you do not have a particular person in mind, let's
approach the character angle from a detective process.

Step One:

Decide what your character looks like. Be
sure to include details.

If you are stumped with his or her looks, start
flipping through some magazines. Cut out
pictures of people you find interesting.
Looking at several models in advertisements
can spark answers to these questions.

Step Two:

Next you'll need to define his/her personality.

Are they angry? Sad? Motivated? A party
animal? Optimistic?
Does he talk to others or keep to themselves?
Does he like music? What kind?
What is his favorite movie?

Step Three:

In order to create some depth for your
character, you'll want to form a history about
him.

Where was he born?
Does he have a family?

Is he educated?
Is there a childhood memory or incident that
has shaped who he is today?

Step Four:

Another item to consider is the motivation of
a character.

He became involved in politics because a law
was not passed when he was young resulting in
the death of a family member.

He was facing a fear of water due to a near
drowning accident when he was young.

He is moving back to Mexico because he
lived there years ago – make sure you give
him a reason as to why Mexico matters to
him.

Step Five:

Make a list containing at least one item or
question for each of the four steps shown
above.

When I took public transportation, I loved it when
there was a delay and I was given the opportunity to
observe my fellow passengers for a short while longer.
When I first observed a passenger, I was careful not to
stare.

Looks

I first made mental notes about his appearance.

- ✓ He had a briefcase with him.
- ✓ He was dressed in jeans and a t-shirt.
- ✓ His hair was cut in a buzz.
- ✓ He was wearing a watch.

Personality

I then spent time deciding what he did for a living and establishing his personality type.

- ✓ He was reading the classified ads section of the newspaper.
- ✓ He was unaware of what was going on around him.
- ✓ He kept looking up to see if he was at his stop.
- ✓ He checked his cell phone a couple of times.

I also based my decision on which stop he got off the bus. It was at an office building area.

History

I created a background based on this information.

- ✓ I gave him a name.
- ✓ I gave him a family since he was wearing a wedding ring.
- ✓ I gave him an occupation.
- ✓ I gave him an age.

✓ I gave him a place of birth.

Motivation

Most bus passenger's motivations were easy to recognize. They were going to work. I decided to focus on his reading of the classified ads.

✓ Was he looking for a new job?
✓ Was he looking for a new car?
✓ Is this why he was taking the bus?
✓ Was he looking for a new place to live?

Topic Detective Time

I gathered some good information with which to build an interesting character background on. I came up with several topics to write about based on this "character."

✦ He was going through a divorce and she got the car.
✦ He was the owner of a company and was looking at the competition.
✦ He was an intense person and was waiting for an important phone call.
✦ His car was totaled and he was looking for a new car.

This passenger gave me enough information to arrive at some conclusions and create a topic.

Conclusion

The benefit of having a person already in mind answers some of the background questions needed to develop a full character. Without having a specific individual in mind, creating a history and motivation for them can generate further topics to write about.

Interviewing individuals for papers can be interesting and entertaining. Remember to take notes about the person's appearance and traits along with the information gathered on the subject.

CHARACTER Exercise

Pick an acquaintance that you don't know very well. It may be someone in a class that sits across the room, or it may be a member of your basketball team. Take a few minutes and come up with a character sketch.

1. Write down what they look like.
2. Write down two personality traits that you have observed.
3. Write down if they have brothers or sisters. If you don't know, decide on your own.
4. Write down why you think they took this class, or play on this team, or ride in the elevator with you once a week.

After you have gathered all this data, write a brief paragraph about who this character is. Remember, you are not recreating the individual, but using them as a base of inspiration to create a fictional character.

Topics are generated by creating a situation that matches the characters unique habits and style.

SETTING

I have discovered in writing this book how many times
I've gone to Las Vegas. I love Las Vegas. Each time I
go, I have a completely different experience than the
time before. I usually stay at a different hotel and each
one is very unique from the hotel next door.

If I wanted to write about Las Vegas, I could base my
idea solely on the premise of the city alone. I wouldn't
need a specific idea or person in mind, the city has a
pulse all its own.

✓ When did it become a twenty-four hour city?
✓ Where do most of its visitors come from?
✓ How did it become known as a wedding
destination?

You may have gone on vacation and thought if you
could bring back the moments in Hawaii or panning
for gold in the Colorado mountains, the setting would
provide a starting point for writing. If you have not paid
attention to background that a setting provides, this
exercise will highlight this detail.

Step One:

Remember a recent vacation. It doesn't have
to be someplace exotic or foreign. It could be
a two hour drive to a campground.

Step Two:

Think about what kind of topics could be written about at this location. Does the location limit the type of ideas available?

Step Three:

How does the location affect the topic idea? Is it because this activity can only occur here?

Step Four:

Why would the location be interesting to your audience?

Step Five:

Write down all of the sensory details about the location. Recall if it was hot or cold, wet or dry, windy or indoors, how did it smell, was it crowded, was it noisy or quiet, either because of nature or man, and any other detail that makes this location distinctive.

I went on a scuba diving trip to Fiji years ago. There are numerous places to scuba dive around the world. I will go through the specifics of Fiji and write why diving here was different than any other place in the world.

My friends and I dived in a place where reef sharks and barracudas swam around at a location in the Blue

Coral Reef called the "zoo." My friends and I watched
the barracudas "mirror" another diver in my group. In
addition to the scuba diving, Fiji also had a local vibe
that I had never experienced anywhere else. I wanted
to talk about other unique events as well.

When we were done diving, we went to dinner where a
local taxi driver slammed on the brakes in the middle
of the road to run out and catch a crab scurrying across
it. He tossed it in the back of the van and we realized
that there were already several crabs tied up in bags
behind the back seat in the taxi mini-van. We kept
looking over our shoulders to make sure the crabs
hadn't gotten loose.

Another day we climbed the side of a mountain to go
down a "waterslide" that was actually slick smooth
rocks that had formed over years from water cascading
over them.

What makes Fiji a good setting is that the Blue Coral
Reef and marine life contained in it doesn't exist
anywhere else in the world. The local culture and
customs are illustrated by telling stories of the taxi
driver and waterfall. These items set the tone and
feeling of where the story is taking place.

Airport

I love going to the airport. It is such a hotbed of
emotions. The setting doesn't have to be about one
particular place. It can be a location where multiple
events occur every minute of every day.

- ✓ People are happy to be meeting someone.
- ✓ They are sad as they are saying goodbye.
- ✓ They can be nervous about being reunited with someone after a long time.

The emotional highs and lows in this location aren't experienced in a grocery store. Sometimes the setting can be about the intangible events as opposed to the physical details.

Extreme Emotion

Picking a location where emotions are pushed to the edge may be a good setting to build an idea around.

- ✓ A bomb squad call.
- ✓ Any police or fire department activity.
- ✓ Finals in a classroom.
- ✓ Giving a speech for the first time.
- ✓ The principal's office where a student is in trouble.
- ✓ A wedding or a funeral.

Inherent to the setting are several story lines that could develop from the circumstances in which the characters find themselves.

High Traffic Areas

Another excellent place for multiple ideas is a setting similar to that of a revolving door.

- ✓ School cafeterias.
- ✓ A hotel lobby.

✓   The food court in a shopping mall.

The object of a good setting is to create a background where all the action can take place and the characters can come to life.

Environment

In non-fiction writing, the setting tells the reader what to expect about the information that will be given in a paper.

If you were given an assignment to write a research paper about the environment, you would want to start with the type of environment.

✓   The forest.
✓   A landfill.
✓   Standing water where mosquitoes or algae grow.
✓   An industrial section of town.

Each of these settings is different from the others. By deciding on the location, the topic will fit the site.

Bathroom

You may also want to pick a setting that you are very familiar with.

✓   Your house.
✓   Your school classroom.
✓   Your car.
✓   The veterinarian.
✓   Your bathroom.

Within the rooms of your house, there are ideas that have already been covered in this book. Think about keeping your topic within the location of your house and not moving outside. You may be surprised how the best ideas can be generated under your own roof.

Let's take the bathroom as an example. Placing a paper or story in a bathroom may seem like an odd idea, so I decided to come up with a few questions that could be specific to the bathroom.

- ✓ How many people sing in the shower?
- ✓ How many people solve problems in the shower?
- ✓ How many people go through the medicine cabinet in someone else's house?

This setting provides topic ideas that cannot be created in any other location. Make sure you don't pick a place that is so unique you are limited to few ideas and come up short on information or storyline.

Topic Detective Time

In using a setting as the source for topics, you will want to answer the basic questions.

- ✓ Where is unique about the location?
- ✓ What kind of action is it, and how does the setting contribute to it?
- ✓ Is there a time frame in which the action needs to occur?
- ✓ Do you want many people around or few?

In asking these questions, I came up with some topics that could be specific to the setting they take place in.

- How is scuba diving in Fiji different than in Hawaii?
- How can a group of friends plan a surprise party in the school cafeteria and keep it a secret?
- Spend a day in a landfill and discover what people toss out.
- In the forest there is no TV. Show the activity in the forest like a TV program.
- How is a firehouse life similar to your home life?
- Why do women go to the bathroom in groups?

Conclusion

Remember, if you only have an idea of where you want to write, that setting can be used as a starting point in creating an entire paper. There has to be a background or backdrop in which the storyline and characters exist.

SETTING EXERCISE

1. Think about where you would like to be right now.

✓ In bed asleep? On a beach listening to the ocean? Watching your favorite band in concert? Running on a track?

2. Next write down some details about the place, either in your mind, or where you are physically located.

✓ Is it hot or cold? Day or night? Are you there by yourself or are other people with you?

3. Why do you want to be there?

✓ You don't have to be responsible for anything, or is it a good vacation memory of a place you want to go back to?

If possible, go to the physical place. If not, pull out photographs and brochures, research it if you don't have a personal memory or if it doesn't exist anymore, or watch movies on the topic or era.

1. Write two questions about the setting that makes it important to what you are writing.
2. What kind of mood or feeling do you want to generate by selecting this setting?
3. Write two memories if it is from an actual experience.

PLOT

There is a story that has been bouncing around in my head for quite some time. The only problem is that the story is not complete. It is really one scene that could be part of several different storylines. I really want to write it, but I don't know where it should go.

Many times a story or idea for an assignment can start from one small thought. If you find yourself in a position where a picture, a scene, or an exchange of dialogue between two characters is all you have in mind, you can still develop it into a full idea.

Step One:

If you have an idea, line of dialogue, character situation, etc. in mind, use it for these steps. If not, think about a time when you were standing in line at the movies.

Step Two:

Think about a conversation you had with your family or friends. Was it about the movie? How long was the line? Who else was there?

Step Three:

Write down a couple of short sentences about what you remember of the dialogue, or what you think the dialogue might have been about.

Make sure your sentence has a person and
some action in it (i.e., she looks like she came
from school)

Step Four:

Pick out your favorite sentence and rewrite it
to make it as short and lean as possible.

Once you have a short, clean sentence, you have a
basic idea for a plot. Your challenge is to take that brief
statement and see how many plot lines you can develop
from it. This exercise will help you create basic story
topics.

Mystery Man

✓ A lone man comes wandering out of the forest.

At first glance, this is a small piece of information. By
asking a few questions, this can be developed into
several topics.

✓ Who is this man?
✓ Why was he in the forest?
✓ Why is he alone?
✓ Where is he heading?
✓ Who is there to see him come out of the
   forest?
✓ Is it day or night?
✓ Is it summer or winter?
✓ Does he have anything in his hands?

The focus of the questions could shift to his appearance, mood, and action.

- ✓ Is he happy, sad, tired, mad, lost, or scared?
- ✓ Does he have a full beard, marking the time frame?
- ✓ Is he carrying a gun, ready to fire?
- ✓ Is he scurrying from tree to tree, keeping cover?
- ✓ Is he on his own, alone with his thoughts?

One sentence could be the catalyst for the story. Perhaps his family has been worried because he disappeared and hasn't been seen for days, months or years.

- ✓ Why did he leave?
- ✓ How has the family changed in the time he's been gone?
- ✓ Are they mad, happy, or sad with his return?

You could take this one statement and turn it into a research or a non-fiction piece.

- ✓ The man has samples from water or soil with him.
- ✓ He has a camera, binoculars, or other observation equipment to report back on industry or poachers.
- ✓ The gun we first see is actually a tranquilizer gun.

The basic mystery outlined in this simple sentence makes it easier to generate topics. The more complex a sentence is, the higher the topic limitations. Remember to take out all qualifiers and descriptions in basic plot topics.

Conversations

I was in a restaurant one day and sitting in the booth next to me were two guys. They were talking about the night before. I overheard the following comment:

- ✓ "When the police showed up, we were in trouble."

Here is a good piece of actual information that can be fictionalized or researched.

Pick a day and research the police calls that came in. Decide if the details on one call look like an interesting plotline. A good example may be a case where the type of call is a response to a party.

- ✓ Where was the party?
- ✓ What did these two guys do to cause the police to show up?

If you want to fictionalize this plot idea, you have a couple of clues to direct your writing.

- ✓ There was more than one person involved when he said "we".
- ✓ At least one person involved is a guy.
- ✓ They were doing something wrong as he said "trouble".

Every conversation is full of clues to write about. Even if you don't hear everything that has been said, this is a case where taking a statement out of context could be fictionalized into a creative exercise.

Make sure you don't try to recreate the event, but use it as inspiration to develop your own unique storyline.

Songs

I was in my car flipping through the radio stations. I stopped at a country western one. I love to hear the stories told in the lyrics.

The song is about a girl who breaks the singer's heart. The song may have been written as a result of a real life relationship, or it could be a story based on others' experiences.

✓ Why does the song talk to you?

Lyrics are full of details, but due to a song's time restriction, there could be more to the story. You could take a song, use the basics to work from and build a complete story around it.

You can listen to the song lyrics, categorize the music into a part of our culture, research the band playing the song, or find out if the song has been previously recorded and discover the song's history.

Cowboys

Country western music makes me think of cowboys. I picture a cowboy and come up with a place.

- ✓ There is a cowboy at a rodeo riding a black bull.

My statement doesn't need to be any longer or detailed. The topic detective in me comes up with these ideas for a plot.

- ✓ Is he riding the bull that he could never beat?
- ✓ Is he ready to retire and this is his last rodeo?
- ✓ Is he a young cowboy and this is his first rodeo?
- ✓ Is the love of his life waiting for him?

Bad versus Good Perspective

Perhaps you have a plot that is based on a place, such as "we went to the lake." You may have visited a lake and thought it was a wonderful time, or your experiences made it a bad place. You can take the lake and develop a full plot from both perspectives.

- ✓ The wildlife around the lake and how the lake provides for it.
- ✓ A family has a picnic there each summer.

The dark side of experiences surrounding a lake could be one of these ideas.

- ✓ A small child drowned in the water.

✓ There is a wedding ring buried in the murky depths.
✓ A wildfire blazes all around the shore line.

Exploring both sides of a plot can enhance your original idea.

Objects

You may also have a plot based on an object. It could be a family heirloom that contains years of history. It could also be an item that is a symbol of love or healing. It could also be an object of mystery.

Something as simple as the coffee table could provide a plot. If I take objects like the remote control, coffee cup, or photo book, I can ask a few questions and come up with a good plot idea.

✓ What was TV life like before the remote?

Okay, what about that coffee cup?

✓ I wonder where the car dealership is located that advertises on side of the cup.

Next, there is an oversized coffee table book on Colorado photos. I flip to a page in the book and wonder about the winter picture.

✓ Was it a blizzard snowstorm in these pictures?
✓ How hard was it to get around in the snow?

Photo books are always excellent sources. You can look at a photograph and decide to write about the picture itself, the events leading up to having the picture taken, or of all the activity that is going on outside of the frame of the photograph.

Topic Detective Time

Having a plot to start from can go in many directions. Based on the ideas generated here, these topics could be written about.

- How many songs are about broken hearts?
- Are broken heart songs more popular in country western music?
- How many peace disturbances are due to parties?
- Is there a night that is more common for these calls? Full moon?
- How much does it vary from police district to district?
- How hard is it to program a universal remote to run everything in my entertainment center?
- I was drinking coffee one day when I swallowed something chunky...
- How many uses are there for a coffee cup?

(A coffee cup could be another multifunction item to brainstorm ideas and topics about.)

- The miner from the 1800s has been reincarnated as my next door neighbor...
- In 1950 when driving over LaVeta pass, the Oldsmobile ran out of gas...

Conclusion

One of the hardest parts of writing a story or paper is
coming up with the initial idea. By stripping out all of
the details and presenting the idea in a basic form,
questions from all angles can be asked. Once the topic
has been developed, the next hardest part is coming up
with a direction to take the topic. In answering
additional questions, various plot lines can be created.

Gathering or creating information from songs, partial
conversations, photos, and simple sentences provide
enough of a foundation to build upon. Once a basic
plot is outlined, filling in the details is an easy task.

PLOT Exercise

Do you have a conversation you'd like to play out? Maybe one you had at school or work. One that didn't go the way you wanted it to. And of course afterwards, you thought of a million things to say.

1. Write down some pieces of the conversation. What someone else said and then what you thought of later to say. After a couple exchanges of dialogue, build a sentence telling what is going on in the conversation (i.e., Max is mad at Christie. Why is he mad?).
2. Once you have your scene, write at least two questions about where the idea could go.
3. Write a question placing the event 20 years down the road - Where are Max and Christie now?

Another way to devise a plot with minimal information is to observe a complete stranger from a distance, across the park, or down the hall. Observe from far enough away that you can't hear their conversation or fully understand what they are doing.

1. Write a statement about what you think they are doing.
2. Write a couple of lines of dialogue of what you think they are saying if they are talking to someone else.

3. Write down where you think they are coming
    from and why they are at this location at this
    time. Create some recent history prior to you
    noticing them, and continue with where you
    think they are going to.

WRITING YOUR MISSION IN THIS WORLD

ASSIGNMENT

Now that you've been given several tools with which to create topics, it is now time to apply them to an actual writing project. In this last section of the book, we will look at different types of papers and writing assignments. By having a variety of topics to choose from, you will be able to pick one that fits the task the best.

RESEARCH

The first writing assignment we are going to cover is the research paper. This could be an assignment that has been given to you in a classroom.

The teacher may assign a specific topic, a range of related topics, or a writer may choose a topic on their own. Regardless, you may use this book and the assignments to generate an topic to satisfy any of these requirements.

I am watching my little sister and think she would make a good topic for a research paper. Her behavior is strange at times, so I think it would be interesting. But writing about her is not a good choice. Why? Even though I may think her behavior is not normal, it has not been documented in any scientific journal or been compared to other girls her age.

I try to come up with ideas that could be used in a paper and still talk about my sister.

- ✓ What makes her odd?
- ✓ What makes her smart?
- ✓ Do other kids her age act the same way?
- ✓ Do other kids her age have the same IQ?

All of these questions can be researched. There is some type of scientific documentation written up in journals of medicine or psychology on these broad questions that give research numbers to support or refute my idea that she is not normal.

Remember when I said having a "character" can spice up a boring research paper? Here is a perfect example. I could start out by listing some of my sister's behaviors in the introduction, and continue to use her to guide the reader through the statistics. By referring back to a "character" as an example, it can help the reader apply and understand the research information better.

Step One:

The number one rule to remember when writing a research topic is choosing one where statistics have been documented and/or information has been collected and organized in **credible publications.**

Step Two:

You will need to decide what type of research format you want to use. Some of the popular

---

types are educating the reader on a subject by approaching it from a historical perspective, compare and contrast, or an argumentative angle where you present the evidence to support your position.

Step Three:

Pick a topic you are interested in!

Since I have a notebook full of ideas from previous chapters, I'm going to sort through them and see which ones would work for a research paper.

Educating the Reader/Historical Information

You can educate the reader on any topic of interest, but when you choose a topic that has historical significance, your paper can focus on the beginning and lead up to the present.

You may pick a topic where the subject is no longer in existence; for example wooden pegs. You can focus your paper on how it affects furniture construction today. I came up with this list of ideas generated earlier:

- ✓ Cedar chest
- ✓ Computers
- ✓ Stuffed animals
- ✓ Pottery
- ✓ Christmas cookies
- ✓ Billboards

All of these ideas are recognizable topics that have been written up in magazines or journals over the years.

Another important consideration in picking a historical topic can be the effects it has had on our culture or society.

Compare/Contrast

If you would rather approach a paper from a comparison and contrast angle, let's go back through the topics developed and see which ones would qualify as having an opposite to consider.

- ✓ The price variation of an unopened toy versus an opened toy.
- ✓ The effects of direct sun versus indirect sun in a room.
- ✓ The differences in US Christmas cookies. versus Ireland Christmas cookies.
- ✓ Learning in a classroom by sitting at desks in rows versus desks in a circle.
- ✓ Individual projects versus group projects.
- ✓ Cramped area versus open area for a home computer space.
- ✓ Noise in the background versus quiet background when at your home computer.

There are other topics that could be reworked to be used as compare and contrast topics, but I found these to be the obvious choices. Remember, when picking a topic with opposite sides, it doesn't mean only two sides exist. Some of these listed topics can be compared and contrasted twenty different ways.

Argument

The third popular research style listed is to present an argument and support your position. To do this, you will need lots of statistics.

If you find a study that supports one angle, look at who did the study and determine if there could be a conflict of interests or a credibility problem.

I am surprised at the drug companies that fund research and then present their findings, which many times support the usage of their drugs. So be careful when using studies. You will want to make sure they are conducted by an unbiased source, like a third party, administering the study.

While grocery store tabloids are very entertaining, they are not recognized as legitimate or factual sources. Research sources need to be credible.

Here are a few topics that I used as examples that would fit this type of research paper.

- ✓ Elementary kids don't need to see their school projects displayed in the school.
- ✓ Public transportation is better than driving your car.
- ✓ Students don't learn when they sit and listen to lectures every day in the classroom.
- ✓ Group projects produce better grades.

- ✓ It is healthy to have sounds in the background when working on a home computer.
- ✓ Personal objects on a desk are distracting.
- ✓ Being a billboard worker is a safe occupation.

As you can see, I had to take topics that were listed in a generic manner and adjust them to a specific position. Remember, when writing a paper using this format, you have to pick a side.

Conclusion

Go back through your exercises that you completed for each chapter and sort out topics which might have documented statistics on them. Then decide which format would best be suited for the topic. Don't be surprised if a topic may be reworked to fit all three formats.

CREATIVE

You may be assigned a creative writing paper. Inherent to anything creative, your imagination is the limit on what you write about. Again, since this is an assignment, you may be given specific topics, a range of topics, or the decision may be left wide open for you to decide.

Step One:

Write about something you are familiar with, something you have experienced, or something you know about.

Step Two:

Pick a topic where you can fictionalize events that may have really happened.

Step Three:
Use all five of the senses to convey a thought or feeling, or you can personify an object. (Personify will be described in this section.)

Step Three:

Pick a topic you like!

Fictionalized Real Events

A real event may not be as interesting as it could be, so by adding fictional drama or additional characters, the event becomes more creative. I went through my topics that could be developed into a complete story.

✓ There were three boys throwing snowballs when I was out walking.

I can create a background on each of these boys and describe a bond that these three form as grade school kids. This would be a fun idea to use as a flashback. One of the boys, who is now a grown adult, comes back to the neighborhood and reunites with his buddies.

✓ Camping in Arizona and fearing the scorpions in my shoes.

This could be one scene from a larger camping trip. I don't recall the rest of the trip, but by building from this one scene, I can write a very comedic event with a family traveling to KOA campgrounds around the southwest.

✓ Planning a party and having a party.

I can use my imagination and create the party of a lifetime. I can include all of the activities I would love to do in real life, but can't due to costs, or location, or guests I want to invite. Creative writing is a great way to live out an experience that is not possible in the real world.

✓ The classroom

Try and change your perspective for the day. Be a teacher in your paper. Imagine what the perfect class lesson would be. Decide who you would invite as a guest speaker and why.

✓ Car glove box

You are driving down the road and you hear a strange sound coming from the glove box. You pull over and open it up. Nothing. Once you start driving again, the sound comes back. It sounds like someone is "knocking" on it, trying to get out.

✓ The TV in the family room.

Write that TV show that you always wanted to see on TV. Make up a fictional actor and tell her story of how she ended up on a TV series.

Using Five Senses

There is nothing better than reading a story where you can use your memory to fill in the blanks. I love reading stories where they describe the warm kitchen and the sweet smell of cinnamon rolls that have just come out of the oven. Can you feel it and smell it?

I went through and picked out two ideal topic candidates for sensory overload.

✓ Christmas

I can hear the crinkling of paper, carols in the backgrounds, and snow crunching under my feet. I can smell pine needles, cookies baking, and hot cider with cinnamon sticks. I can see twinkling lights in the trees that line the road.

You can write anything you want about this holiday or any other holiday that has strong sensations associated with it.

✓ Riding the Bus

There was a guy in one of my classes who wrote about the people riding the bus with him. He used a ton of description. I felt like I was on the bus with him.

I could smell the exhaust and feel the hot sun burning my arm through the window. I could see the bus stop at each corner, trash on the street, advertising on the bus shelter walls and sound of music that could only be half heard through the headphones of the guy sitting in the next seat.

The reader can experience the ride with you while drawing on his own memories.

Personification

We haven't talked about this style of writing, but I'm sure you have seen it before. Take an object and give it human-like qualities. I went through my list and came up with a good inanimate object to make human.

✓ The shoes in my closet.

Instead of being a pair of shoes, they became characters. I named one shoe Harry and the other shoe Charlie. They went on a trip to the grocery story and Harry stepped into some gum. Charlie spent half of the time trying to disassociate himself with Harry since Harry couldn't seem to keep his sole out of trouble.

Charlie is a really nice shoe, and Harry is the problem shoe in the pair. Harry's troublemaking style all started when he was separated right after manufacturing from Charlie. He spent a fair amount of time in his young days all alone, until he was paired up with Charlie once again.

Sounds ridiculous, right? Maybe, but it is a fun way to look at your shoes in a whole new light. Go back through your items and see which ones would make interesting characters.

Conclusion

When you look at the exercises completed in each section, look at the types of questions you came up with. Creative writing may be the answer.

- ✓ It tells the story of a person.
- ✓ It tells the story of an event.
- ✓ It tells the story of a family.
- ✓ It tells the story of the future or past.
- ✓ It tells a mystery or a comedy.
- ✓ It teaches a lesson.

The only thing you need to remember, be creative and write something you like.

DOCUMENTATION

Another type of writing is documentation. Many families are starting to document family histories in formal ways by recording family stories that can be told for generations to come. Other families want to document one particular moment in life. Families are capturing family reunions and keeping track of family roots and distant relatives. Two of the more common ways to do this are a memoir or a non-fiction account.

MEMOIR

I have been to the bookstore and looked up memoirs. Many are written by people in the music and film industry and others are written by people I have never heard of. If I don't recognize the author's name, I read the back of the book and discover the story they tell.

Some authors have been fighter pilots in a war, some have learned about life by surviving the death of a loved one, others have written about how a sister changed their life. All of these stories have one thing in common: they are all written from a first person narrative.

> **Step One:**
>
> Write about something you have experienced. Use "I" because you are telling it *first person*.

> ### Step Two:
>
> This reflection should either be an account of your life so far or about an event that has affected you deeply.
>
> ### Step Three:
>
> Pick a topic that is personal, but not so personal that you don't want to share it.

While it may be common that three people experience the exact same event in three different ways, a memoir recounts the narrator's memories only.

Some of the topics generated earlier that could be memoirs would be:

- ✓ The adventures of camping in my family.
- ✓ My parents divorce announcement at the kitchen table.

When looking at the topics that were created in each section, there may not be one that stands out as a memoir. I feel that memoir writing comes from deep within a writer.

There are two main reasons why a writer wants to tell their story:

One is the author has learned something from an experience and wants to share their knowledge with the public.

The other is, I think, a mood or feeling living inside the writer, and the writer decides it needs to be told.

Conclusion

The level of personalization in a memoir is high. The level of emotion is high. You may not feel like you have experienced enough in your life at this point to write a memoir, but you'd be surprised at how many life experiences you have already had. Any experience that has caused you to grow as a person can be told in a memoir. Don't discount your age as a factor in this section.

NON-FICTION

One of the more common ways to document a family story is to write an event from a less personal perspective. This is a non-fiction paper.

Non-fiction writing may surround a person or a single event, or it may be a more involved non-fiction account that describes an era, or a country, or a people.

Writing a non-fiction paper isn't as personal as a memoir. It is telling the story as close to the facts as may be told. Some of it may seem personal if you are telling a story involving your family, but when you collect data, you are acting more like a reporter or historian than writing an extension of yourself.

A family interview can be a fun and interesting paper to write. You may discover something new about your ancestors.

Step One:

Pick an event that may be researched.

Step Two:

Interview the people who were involved in the event.

Step Three:

Pick a topic that other readers can relate to.

Some good topics for a non-fiction event would be:

- ✓ My grandmother's move to the west.
- ✓ What school was like for my grandmother and what lessons were taught to her.
- ✓ The distant relative who built the rocking chair and other furniture that was built at the time.

These topics are about how events affected people you may know, but you weren't around when it happened. You are, however, certainly affected by the outcome of the event.

Conclusion

Non-fiction is similar to a research paper with the inclusion of statistics and results from studies. By stating my grandmother was one of thousands who traveled west that year, I can include statistical information to support her personal story. It always adds credibility to the reporting nature of non-fiction to back up statements with hard data.

I could treat my grandmother like a character. It may not seem as obvious in non-fiction pieces, but if I wanted to write a research paper on traveling, focusing on my grandmother's travels could make the research more colorful. Your audience would relate to the individual easier than to the generic topic of travel.

JOURNALING

Journaling is a good practice to get used to the idea of writing on a regular basis. The nice thing about journaling is its flexibility. Two major forms of journaling are for personal reasons and for assignment reasons.

PERSONAL

With journaling, you may cover events and feelings of your daily life. Many view their journal as a friend and companion. For some, it is the only way to turn off the flow of thoughts bouncing around day after day in the mind. I have discovered that it's true! Once the problem or feeling is written on paper, the mind can clear itself and move on!

<u>Step One:</u>

Get a notebook and carry it around with you for the day.

<u>Step Two:</u>

If you think of an idea or even a short sentence, write it down.

> ### Step Three:
>
> Try this for a week and see how many ideas you discover.

While much personal journaling is done for meditative reasons, many writers will journal to capture the idea or feeling of a moment. They like to go back and review what they've written to put it to use for a future character, storyline, or research idea. If you find that you are one who, even after completing all the exercises in this book, still can't decide what to write about, journaling may be something to try.

There are virtually no restrictions, unless you choose to place them on yourself. The stress of coming up with a specific number of pages, or specific topic by a specific date, is non-existent. The mind has a chance to be creative all on its own.

There are different ways to journal. Some people prefer the pen and paper route in a spiral notebook. They can jot down a sentence or paragraph several times throughout the day. Others like the keyboard. Laptops are ideal for having around and turning on throughout the day. If a desktop is all you have, setting time aside for nothing but "what rolls off the top of your head" writing can be the way to go.

Another popular way to journal is to "blog" on the internet. Many sites offer free memberships. You have the ability to set up a personal profile, link to your friends, and receive feedback from those who read your journal entries online.

Those who struggle with being creative have been shocked when pieces of a plot come together on a page. Others have identified a specific personality trait and use it to build a character. Yet others want to record a specific moment, like a vacation incident, and don't want to forget the details. There's nothing worse than looking at pictures a month later and already forgetting where the picture was taken.

The nice thing about trying this is if you find you don't want to write anything that day, you don't have to. If you find this is too relaxed, set aside some writing time each day. It may be as short as ten minutes right before you go to sleep.

I can't list any topics to help you out with this writing section. The whole purpose is to let the mind go and let the words flow. I highly recommend that if you haven't tried journaling, give it a chance. Even with all of the other information you will get from this book, you will surprise yourself at how unstructured writing can create a world within your world.

ASSIGNMENT

Now that we've covered the personal aspect of journaling, how can this activity be assigned? There are psychology class students who keep journals as they interview people, study the general population, or for other activities assigned in the course. Teachers have found that the psychology behind journaling takes pressure off the student and better information is gathered in this form of documentation.

Like a paper assignment, the journal is turned in and a grade is given. There is usually more structure given to this type of journaling, like the number of entries for each day or each week, and the information that needs to be included in an entry. It is still completed by the student without the formality of being a term paper or research paper.

English classes may use journaling assignments to get the student in the habit of writing every day. When I was in the eighth grade, I had an English teacher who told us we had to write in a class journal for ten minutes every day. The class was shocked and panicked at the thought! Ten minutes felt like a lifetime, but it started me on the path of writing. I am eternally grateful to that eighth grade teacher!

What I thought was an impossible task at first made me tap into my creative mind. The teacher gave us the challenge and told us that if we wrote "I don't know what to write" over and over again on the page, sooner or later we'd tire of the sentence and think of something better to write. I don't know what the others did, but I thought about writing a soap opera. Each day would be an installment in the storyline.

I felt pretty silly at the beginning, but when I found myself thinking of adventures that my characters could have next, I realized journaling was important. It got to the point where I couldn't wait to write the next installment in class the next day.

When starting a soap opera type of story, your idea could be something as basic as:

- ✓ Adventures in taking the bus and what happens each day on the streets outside the window.
- ✓ Charlie and Harry, the shoe adventures.
- ✓ Dream vacation adventures based on the pictures tacked up at your computer.
- ✓ Character sketches and bios for another writing project.

If you get a journaling assignment, remind yourself that the structure is easier than a paper. Relax and let your thoughts flow onto the page. Remember that for a journaling assignment you will write about subjects that the teacher is likely going to read. Don't write anything too personal.

ORGANIZATION

Writing is one of the best ways to organize your thoughts. You can put it in an outline form, you can cut and paste paragraphs together, you can delete pages from a paper, or you can play with words that convey a thought or feeling better.

The two most common reasons for organizing your thoughts in writing are for speeches and for therapy. These are two completely different experiences, but both benefit from organization.

SPEECH

One of the most important moments to be organized is when giving a speech or important address to an audience. I can always tell when a speaker has not written out their thoughts. Without organization, he has a tendency to jump from point to point, back up when he realizes he forgets something important, talk in circles and keep repeating the same information. He also goes off on a tangent that has nothing to do with the topic originally presented.

By planning, in writing, the introduction, the important details, and the conclusion, a speaker is usually more comfortable. He knows what he's doing up there! While many say they would rather have a root canal than stand up in front of others, organizing and planning a speech, in writing, may at least save you some stress!

Step One:

Pick a topic the audience can relate to. Pick one that every person sitting in your audience has probably experienced at least once in their lifetime.

Step Two:

Pick a topic that fits one of these formats, informational, persuasive, or compare and contrast. These are some of the most common types of speeches given.

Choosing a Topic

I was sitting in speech class listening to a student talk about the differences between gutting a rainbow trout versus gutting a northern pike fish. I'd never been fishing, never had the desire or the interest to gut a fish, and 90% of what the speaker said went in one ear and out the other. He brought in gory overhead pictures to support his comments which further pushed me into my own thoughts.

Keep in mind that what may rock your world may not even be a spark in someone else's. Be aware of the reason you are speaking. It's to communicate with your audience. If you lose them in the first minute, you aren't achieving your goal. Here are some topics that I think would work well:

- ✓ Where do I rent a DVD? Who has the best selection, the best snacks to go with it, and best prices?
- ✓ Getting lost driving somewhere. Are people landmark oriented, street oriented, or mileage oriented? What's the best way to give directions?
- ✓ What is the best way to study for a test, and how can you determine which way works best for you?
- ✓ Which is the best home computer? What are the most popular games? What is the best internet service for the cheapest price?

All of these topics are general enough that chances are you will be speaking to everyone in the room. If the audience can't relate to what you're saying, chances are they won't listen.

Question What You Are Saying

If you are writing a speech that debates an issue and you want to be persuasive in gaining the support of others, pick a topic that has two clear sides. In one speech class, I used the existence of UFOs as my topic. While half the class never looked at me the same way again, I was successful in gaining the votes of a few students.

I would not have had any success with my speech had I not laid out my thoughts and looked for holes in my argument. This is the place to think about all angles of your argument and ask yourself the questions that others may ask you.

Practice Saying it Aloud

When making any verbal presentation, read it aloud. Make sure you are saying what you are thinking. You may not have a piece of paper to refer back to and "read between the lines" in a presentation. You have to present all the information up front and use strong words to get your point across.

The other main reason to read aloud is to make sure you are comfortable with the topic. I will never forget being in a speech class where a student got up to tell the story of a sibling who died of cancer. This difficult topic to listen to was even more difficult as the speaker was not able to get through the presentation. It was awkward for the entire class. The speaker got a low grade because half of her presentation was unintelligible.

Conclusion

Subject matter needs to be chosen carefully with the audience in mind. If you want to talk about interior decorating, the football club may not be an appropriate choice of audience. Go back through the exercises and look at your responses. Think about them as ideas for speech topics.

THERAPY

Another way to use writing to organize your thoughts is to help you work out a strong emotion or emotional occurrence. I have been so angry at a person that I couldn't see straight. After storming away from the scene, I am left with my thoughts. When this happens, I sit down and write out what I think happened.

<u>Step One:</u>

There are no steps to this writing.

A lot of people use writing as therapy. As I mentioned before, when an idea is spinning around in your mind and you want to break free from it, write it down. The same is true here. If you are sad, mad, or feeling any other emotion, write it down. I have found there are times that, after I write it down, I see things differently and realize it wasn't as bad as it seemed at the time.

<u>Having a Plan</u>

In making a phone call or a face-to-face visit with someone who has caused uncomfortable feelings in me, I may find that writing down my thoughts helps to better express my feelings. Just as in the speech process, having a plan to follow in stating my position, telling why I feel the way I do, and what I hope will come out of this conversation, may make the exchange go smoother.

Arguments

I have been in arguments where I did no planning and
I kept talking in circles. Not only did the problem not
get solved, it created a bigger one. Had I written down
why I was mad, the other person involved would have
been better informed, knew what I expected of them,
and the argument would have had a point.

When Writing Doesn't Help

If there is an occasion where the feeling doesn't
subside, writing may not be the solution. Talking to
someone may be your best action. Don't treat it like an
embarrassment or sign of weakness to ask for help.
Everyone needs someone to listen to them at times in
their life.

Conclusion

Of course, many times there is no opportunity to write
down your thoughts and organize them until later. This
section is really about where a situation has already
happened and you are trying to figure it out. Writing
for this purpose is really about three things:

- ✓ clearing your mind of repeating thoughts
- ✓ defining what the problem really may be
- ✓ deciding how you want to present your
  experience to others

There are no topics that can be listed for this section.
This form of writing is for you to personalize based on
your needs.

EDUCATION

All books teach us something. It could be facts about another country told through a spy thriller, or the basics of the game of golf written by an expert in the field. Books may teach us about ourselves when we discover a character that reminds us of ourselves.

When a connection is made, we can grow from the reading experience and discover something new in our personality. While most books teach us a variety of subjects, for the purposes of this book I'm going highlight two areas: Children's and How-To books. You may not realize the wealth of knowledge you have already obtained in life. This is an opportunity to highlight your knowledge and share it with others.

Step One:

Pick a topic that you know well. You may not think of yourself as an expert on a topic, but don't sell yourself short. You are an expert in anything you do daily.

Step Two:

Decide on a category you would like to write about, either Children's or How-To.

Step Three:

Think about your audience and what would
be an age-appropriate subject.

Step Four:

Outline your topic so you have a clear plan in
teaching your subject.

I chose to put educational books in their own section
because it requires a creative angle to make an
educational topic interesting.

Children's Books

I love early children's books. I love how they are so
simple in their messages, but so complex the way they
are put together. It took some creative thinking to
come up with the idea of three pigs living in houses
made of different materials. It teaches us about house
construction, family, numbers, and right or wrong.

You may be a fan of children's books and want to write
to this audience. If so, keep in mind that many books
in this genre teach basics along with entertainment.

- ✓ numbers
- ✓ colors
- ✓ addition and subtraction
- ✓ how to identify objects
- ✓ families and relations

Some use the basics in multiple ways. Say a book is about colors. The author may name the characters Ms. Peach or Mr. Blue. The author may cross over the colors into alliteration. Alliteration is using the same letter numerous times in one sentence. For example, Ms. Peach likes purple plums. The child is learning to say the letter P several times in a row.

Besides the cleverness of children's book from this perspective, many books also teach stories about the town you live in. They may explain the difference between an airport and a train station. A younger sibling, for example, could benefit from a homemade book based on your experience of an airplane ride.

Personification is popular in Children's books. Using topics generated earlier and personifying the object could make a fun writing experience.

- ✓ Shoes. Take a child on an adventure through her closet and count up the shoes present. This could teach numbers and math.
- ✓ Family Pet. Take the pet on a tour of the neighborhood and introduce it to other pets along the way. This could introduce a child to new animals.
- ✓ Christmas Ornaments. Take a child on a holiday adventure as the ornament meets other ornaments on the tree. This could teach several holiday stories as each ornament tells what they represent.
- ✓ Family Car. Take a child on a trip around the city or state. This could teach geography.

How-To Books

Researching a subject is necessary to educate a reader in how to do something, but these books benefit more from the author's personal experience. Browse through any bookstore and try to locate all the types of books that educate us on how to do something.

- ✓ How to fix leaky sinks.
- ✓ How to fix a broken heart.
- ✓ How to fix a car.
- ✓ How to fix a computer.

When choosing a topic to teach to others, it is important that the author have a focus. A good outline will lay out the plan of how to teach the reader. You don't want to teach a reader how to fly a kite by telling them to toss it into the wind. You'll need to teach them to make sure they have the string attached first.

Good topics developed earlier could be focused on writing how to do something that affects your friends.

- ✓ How to select the best prom shoes.
- ✓ How to decorate your home computer.
- ✓ How to plan a party.
- ✓ How to be a member in a school group project.
- ✓ How to read a bus schedule.
- ✓ How to accessorize a car.

By asking the question "how do I" with any topic, you can decide if it would be a good educational idea.

Conclusion

It can be a fun memory exercise to recall something unique or unusual about your family or neighborhood. Teaching a child this memory and educating them in the process can be a rewarding experience. You may remind yourself how much you really do know!

The same can be said about "How-To" writing. You are an expert in many things. Once you recognize a topic and follow through your step-by-step process in teaching it, you will be surprised at the complexities involved when learning an activity.

EXPRESSIONS

I have had many occasions to write a thoughtful message to a friend in sad times and in happy times. Many people keep cards and letters for years. Love letters have been recovered from trunks in attics years after the deaths of the couple involved. Christmas cards dating back forty years were discovered in boxes in my mom's closet. Those cards with written notes and letters were treasured by her.

> ### Step One:
>
> There are no steps to this writing.

You can express a feeling in any form you see fit, but I have come up with a couple of categories for you to consider.

- ✓ Poetry
- ✓ Cards
- ✓ Song Lyrics

We'll start off with poetry as the other two categories are different ways to represent poetic writing.

Poetry

I love writing poetry. There isn't a better way to capture a snapshot of life than by writing a descriptive stanza using colorful language. Half the fun of writing poetry is finding the right words to convey a feeling or emotion.

You may write about something as simple as watching a leaf fall from a tree. Poems don't have to be long. Some of the best ones contain two or three lines. Other poems can last five pages. The freedom allowed in poetry gives the writer an opportunity to express her personal style with few restrictions.

Poetry can follow a particular format, such as rhyming words, or a specific design like haiku, or you can write from the heart in free verse. Free verse doesn't follow any guidelines except for your words of expression on a page.

Topics popular in poetry can range as far as the imagination can wander.

- ✓ Your dream vacation.
- ✓ Your pet.
- ✓ The lint on your bedroom carpet.
- ✓ A stuffed animal in the rocking chair.
- ✓ The time on the clock.
- ✓ Your dream car.

Just remember, when writing poetry, play with the words you use. The more colorful the words, the more colorful the poem.

Greeting Cards

Another way to express yourself is by creating a card. With computer software easily available, anyone can create cards for any occasion. You can add pictures and then write a snappy line of quick wit inside that illustrates your feelings and no one else's.

I created a card that had a picture of a stack of pennies on the cover and inside a clever line about keeping track of money. You could use the same stack of pennies and write an inspirational line about starting small and growing big. You always have to start somewhere, right?

The key to writing a card is to think about who the card is for. Think about your audience and pick a topic that they like.

If they like dogs, put a picture of their dog or a dog breed they like on the cover and on the inside you could write something like:

You're like a bone in the backyard. I leave you alone for a week and when I come back, you're still there.

Best friends...

One of the best ways to generate a topic for a card is to find a photo. By choosing a picture with friends or family or a pet, you may discover an expression, or detail, that can generate a few lines of poetic writing.

I was writing about some childhood photos and realized upon further inspection that what I thought was a picture of my birthday party was really a picture of my dad's birthday. I was a three year old child "helping" him open up boxes.

Each time I glanced at these pictures in the box of old photos, I jumped to conclusions. When I decided to write about it, I realized that the photo told the true story. I just hadn't been paying attention.

Topics mentioned earlier that could be used in greeting cards include:

- ✓ Family - vacation pictures, sports events, hobbies
- ✓ Friends - parties, music events, gossip

Song Lyrics

Perhaps you are the musical type. I can't help but talk about country western songs once again. They make my eyes tear up over broken hearts and then make me laugh over broken dishwashers all in one line. What a wonderful expression of life.

If it's easier for you to imagine music in your presentation, than writing to a melody may be the way to create a topic. I like to think of lyrics as poetry set to music.

Conclusion

These are several ways to show expressions in writing. You don't need to write a lengthy paper for these writing expressions. You can write a line or two and get your message across. The more creative, the more it will be remembered in years to come.

MISCELLANEOUS

I decided to group these last few items together under a miscellaneous category. They may not be considered writing assignments for a class, but they are writing projects that you may benefit from.

WRITE A MOVIE

Every good movie starts with an idea. Before an actor or director is attached to a movie project, the movie professionals have to like the idea. It is called in the movie industry, the "pitch" of the movie idea. The key to picking a good screenplay topic is the conflict in the story. It can be conflict between the characters, a character and the setting, or a conflict within the character.

You may discover that you like playing out conversations between people in your mind. There may be one line of dialogue that bounces around in your brain from time to time. You may also discover that a story or paper written for an assignment may play out well on a screen.

I wrote a short story in an English class one time. I could visualize each scene of the story. I finally realized the dialogue and storyline could convert into a screenplay.

Step One:

Pick a topic that has conflict in it.

Step Two:

Create characters to showcase your story through their dialogue.

Step Three:

Decide on a setting where the conflict is going to take place.

Watch some of your favorite movies. Watch it with a detective's eye. Why is the movie good?

- ✓ Characters?
- ✓ Dialogue?
- ✓ Storyline?
- ✓ Mood, feeling, tone?
- ✓ Action, stunts?
- ✓ Special effects?

All of these items contribute to the topic.

Conflict

I went back through the topics discovered and picked out ones that had a storyline involving conflict within them.

- ✓ Four wheel driving to a destination.

- ✓ A young couple marrying in the depression – cedar chest given as a gift, generations later and whom the cedar chest has been handed down to.
- ✓ Christmas (writer's choice of any topic)
- ✓ Best friends in school and their competing science projects.
- ✓ A girl with bulimia and her brother who tries to save her.

The types of conflict in each of these could be categorized as the main character needs to solve a problem, or work through a problem, or defeat a problem.

- ✓ The driver of a four wheel car could be in conflict with the elements of nature.
- ✓ The cedar chest could represent a conflict of lifelong expectations and those that fell short and how the main character has to resolve this.
- ✓ The school friends could be conflicted with wanting to win, but not at the expense of their friendship.
- ✓ The girl with bulimia has conflict with the illness.
- ✓ Christmas doesn't come this year for a little boy due to being caught throwing snowballs.

Characters

With screenplays, just like with any other creative project, the sky is the limit in choosing a topic. In the topics mentioned in the last section, you need to make sure there is an interesting character to star in it.

Writing about a pinecone would not be all that interesting on the screen. Writing about a family occurrence, or a holiday festivity, or friends includes excellent character examples.

In the examples above the characters are:

- ✓ The driver who wants to beat Mother Nature.
- ✓ The grandmother who planned on being married forever.
- ✓ The boy in school who wants to help his best friend.
- ✓ The girl who tries to cover up her illness.
- ✓ The boy who can't seem to stay out of trouble.

Setting

These examples also include very specific settings. Sometimes the setting can be considered another character in a screenplay. This is true with the first example. By having the driver compete with Mother Nature, she is the focus of the conflict.

Settings for the other examples are the home and a classroom.

Formatting

If you want to write a screenplay, there are specific rules for formatting a screenplay. I suggest researching a few books on screenwriting and familiarizing yourself with the nuts and bolts. The book I recommend is David Trottier's The Screenwriter's Bible.

Conclusion

By having a couple of characters work out a topic that
has conflict, you may create a good movie idea may be
created. Keep this in mind when you go back through
your exercises to see which of your topics could be
converted into a screenplay.

ENTER A CONTEST

Many writing organizations offer writing contests for the genre they support. Some of the best entrants in these contests are papers you've completed for a class. Writing assignments have been edited, work-shopped or revised many different times. You always want to enter your best work in contests.

Step One:

Pick a topic.

Step Two:

Come up with a unique or different angle to the topic.

Contests can be tricky. Many times the words "fresh" and "provocative" are used when describing what the judges look for in an entry. The writer is now challenged with the task of taking an idea that has been written about before and finding a new angle on it.

In an English class in college, the professor told us that we couldn't write papers on certain topics because he was tired of reading them several times over. I chose UFOs and much to his dismay, he neglected to include this on his list! He gave me the opportunity to present my paper on UFOs from a fresh angle. If I could do that, he would approve it.

I went home and wrote down every question I could think of regarding UFOs. One of my questions was:

✓ Who believes in UFOs?

Based on this question I came up with a topic of people who are already paranoid were more likely to believe in UFOs because UFOs are a result of psychology related disorders. He accepted the paper and I received an A.

Regardless of the type or style of entry, whether it's a poetry submission or a short story, if you can create a unique slant on a topic, you have a greater opportunity of placing or winning the contest.

In looking at some of the ideas created earlier, I analyzed a couple of them and tried to come up with a different perspective on the topic.

✓ Christmas – the difference between Santa Claus and St. Nicholas.
✓ Camping – in a science fiction world where time travel occurs every hour.

Conclusion

The process of finding different perspective on topics is difficult to work through. This is probably the second biggest hurdle for a writer to cross, the first hurdle being finding a topic to write about.

Write silly questions, dumb questions, and bizarre questions. If you can ask enough questions about a topic, you can come up with something that is not completely ordinary. The more creative the notes on your paper, the better your chances are that you'll brainstorm a different approach.

GIVE A GIFT

On my best friend's birthday, I took years of photographs and wrote everything I could remember about those times. I stapled, cut, and glued the pictures and pages together, placed them in an emptied CD case, and made a mock music cover for the front and back. At first she thought she was getting a new CD of her favorite band. She was surprised when she opened it and saw all of our memories displayed inside.

The theme of the gift is important. As an example, I have seen western themed memories bound between two pieces of wood and a piece of barbed wire. The fun of giving this type a gift is to turn the words into a presentation.

Step One:

Whom is the gift for?

Step Two:

Decide the reason for the gift, if there is one.

Step Three:

Look at what the recipient's interests are. Don't forget this is a gift about her and for her. You may have a tendency to give something you like, instead of what she likes.

Step Four:

Think of a creative presentation for your
words and pictures.

If the gift is for your brother who played football, you
could shape the pages like a football. If the gift is for
your Aunt Hilda who loves knitting, bind it with yarn,
or, if she taught you how to knit, knit the covers and
place the pages inside.

The gift could be for a birthday. Tell the birthday
person the history of birthdays and why his is
important. Another idea is to put together your own
historical information of the year he was born.
Personalize the history with facts about his family,
where he was living at the time, or other information
gathered from family or close friends.

If the gift is to commemorate each Christmas that is
spent at grandmother's house, you could put together a
Christmas book that highlights what makes her special
or how she makes the holiday special.

Gifts can be a mix of writing styles. A friend once asked
me to help her put together a gift for her daughter's
graduation from college. My friend had a poem in
mind, but couldn't figure out where to go from there.
So, we started off the book with her poem. The next
pages were papers her daughter had completed
throughout her school years. My friend then wrote
some of her memories about her daughter and her
daughter's milestones in school.

This gift was part poetry, part research paper, and part memoir. By using all of these writing styles, the gift had personal reflections and historical data. My friend's daughter was surprised that her mom had kept her school papers. It illustrated her school achievements even more.

When picking a topic for a gift, it's all about the recipient. The gift should be:

- ✓ memories that she is a part of
- ✓ to commemorate something she has accomplished or is celebrating

Conclusion

By choosing something that focuses on the recipient's tastes, you can make a personal item that will be appreciated more than a store bought item.

Remember to write a few words from the heart. It will be a gift they never forget.

Finale

Do you feel more creative? Do you recognize your lifetime of ideas? Do you think you can create better topics from those ideas?

It is my hope that at least one type of exercise was something your creative brain could tap into. Since many people learn by different methods, one of these sections should be able to help you.

I also hope that you realize how much you have done in life. Travels to exotic locations or cloak and dagger activities aren't the only topics to write about.

I've included many types of writing formats, but there are many more that could be taught in a class or included in other lessons. Don't treat this book as an ending place in your writing challenges. This book is meant to spark creativity and help you begin to grow as a writer.

By looking at an object from a curious perspective, and developing questions as to why an object exists, where an object came from, or who uses the object, will give you plenty of writing choices.

Congratulations!
You are now a certified topic detective!

Index

Quick Order Form

Fax orders: 720-488-5255. Fax this form.
Email orders: orders@citylifebooks.com or
www.citylifebooks.com and use shopping cart
Postal orders: City Life Books, PO Box
371136, Denver, CO 80237 USA

Please send the following book. I understand
that I may return it for a full refund, for any
reason, no questions asked.

☐ **Creating Ideas: Discover Writing Topics in
Daily Life**

Name: _____

Address: _____

City: _____ State: _____
Zip: _____

Telephone: _____

email address: _____

Sales tax: Please add 6.45% for products
shipped to Colorado addresses.

Shipping by air:
US: $4.00 for first book, $2.00 each additional.
International: $9.00 for first book, $5.00 for
each additional.

Payment: ☐ Check   ☐ Money Order   ☐
Credit Card: ☐ Visa   ☐ Mastercard
            ☐ American Express

Card Number:
_____Exp._____
Mailing Address Zip Code: _____
Name on Card: _____